Welcome To My World!

A week in the life of a substance abuse counselor

A Novel by

Mary Crocker Cook, D.Min., LMFT, LPCC, LAADC, CADCII

Welcome to My World

© 2014 Mary Crocker Cook

ISBN: 978-1-61170-169-2

Published in the USA.

 Robertson Publishing™
www.RobertsonPublishing.com

Printed in the USA, UK, and Australia on acid-free paper.

To purchase additional copies go to:
  amazon.com
  barnesandnoble.com

Welcome to My World is a product of my imagination and in no way depicts specific counselors and staff from my treatment center experience. The characters are a composite, and I suspect will be familiar to those who share my love of treatment and alcohol and drug counselors.

I have provided a weekly schedule for readers who may be unfamiliar with the day-to-day structure of treatment. As you are reading you might be struck by the pace of the day, and I assure you this pace is very real! I have also illustrated specific groups that take place during the week to provide a window into the treatment world.

With many thanks to my editor, Howard Scott Warshaw, LMFT

—Mary Crocker Cook

PROLOGUE

Janet leans forward, resisting her instinct to brush Matt's hair out of his eyes, and says, "I know you think you have a handle on this. And I am afraid for you, because guys like you die if you don't let us help you."

Matt is quiet a moment, gives her a reassuring smile, and says, "You don't need to worry. I love my family and I would never let that happen."

Two months later Janet receives notice that Matt died of alcohol poisoning. She sighs, then goes to the door to meet the next client.

A week in the life of a substance abuse counselor

Daily Schedule

	M	T	W	TH	F	Sat	Sun
7:00-8:30	Wake/ brkfst	Wake/ brkfst	Wake/ brkfst	Wake/ brkfst	Wake/ brkfst	Wake/ brkfst	Wake/ brkfst
8:30-9:00	Mindful-ness	Mind.	Mind.	Mind.	Mind.	Mind.	Mind.
9:00-10:00	Women/ Men's Group	Yoga	Nutrition	DBT	Assign-ment Group	Family only	Free
10:15-11:00	Comm Group	Comm. Group	Comm. Group	Comm. Group	Comm. Group	10:30-11:45 Multi-family	Double Scrub
11:30-12:30	Psychoed	Psych'd	Psych'd	Psych'd	Psych	12:00 Lunch	
12:30-1:45	Lunch/ Staff mtg	Lunch	Lunch	Lunch	Lunch	Visit	Lunch
2:00-3:30	Process Group	Process	Process	Art Therapy	Process	Visit	
3:30-5:00	Free					3:00 Visiting over	4:00 Outside meeting
5:00-6:00	Dinner						
6:00-6:30	After Dinner clean-up						Dinner
6:30-8:00	Psychoed	Psych'd	Psych'd	Psych'd	Psych'd	H&I Meeting	
8:00-9:00	Chores	Chores	Chores	Chores	Chores	Chores	Chore
9:00-11:00	Free						

MONDAY

As Janet, the lead CD counselor, enters her office on Monday she checks the weekend log notes for any issues left over from family group or incidents between residents that need follow-up. She notices there is a note about the new admit, Karen, on Sunday. The staff log is the written record of day to day activities that each shift uses to communicate with each other. They report comings and goings, drops offs, new admissions, client incidence reports, client consequences, and left over tasks to be completed from the previous shifts. The log is a key document and the focus of a lot of client speculation, because clients count on poor communication between staff in order to run game and manipulate the system.

When she feels caught up, Janet listens to her voice mail and picks up a message from her primary counselor, Ricardo, who is calling in late with his usual 'Jerry Springer' drama. This leaves his clients hovering around her desk, vying for attention with her own caseload. She stuffs down her resentment with a donut as she signs Andrew's medical pass and makes a quick phone call to Karen's probation officer. She notices the clock ticking quickly toward Women's group, and hears the impatient footsteps of the Clinical Director who has arrived early to cover Men's group in Ricardo's absence.

Women's Group

Janet looks around the circle during the women's group and notices Karen, the new group member. As she introduces herself, she sees the tension in Amanda's torso as Amanda bends forward slightly and wraps her arms protectively across her abdomen.

"Amanda, you seem to be having a hard time," Janet notices.

Amanda appears to have trouble catching her breath, and the tears begin to slide down her face as she slowly begins to rock. Fighting the urge to hug Amanda (which would interrupt her) Janet gently coaxes, "Amanda, honey. How can we help you?"

Through a curtain of hair Amanda cries, "My mom called and my CPS worker has denied my reunification because I needs to be clean from meth longer before I can get Joey back."

Janet knows Amanda has put all of her hopes in this decision, and this is a crucial point in Amanda's recovery. Janet can feel the rustle of the other addicted mothers in the room as they resonate with Amanda's grief and disappointment.

Josie, next in the circle, puts her arm around Amanda, who leans in to cry on her shoulder. This is especially powerful because Josie lost her 3 children to a custody battle 15 years ago and has drowned her grief in drugs and alcohol ever since. Amanda's mother died when she was very young, and she was raised by a resentful grandmother and distant father. Amanda desperately needs nurturing, and Josie's ability to care for the younger woman is balm for her grieving soul. Josie is able to provide the soothing that Janet's professional role does not allow, even though Janet knows this is what the young woman needs most right now.

The other women gently take turns sharing their experience with Amanda, encouraging her that being clean and sober will eventually restore her family. "It just seems so slow, and feels so hard to have supervised visits and to have to leave him when he's crying for me!" she says against Josie's shoulder.

"And the worst part..." Amanda sputters though her tears, "it's my fault Joey's sad! Sometimes I wish I could use again just for a while so I can forget the sad look on his face when I leave."

The women around her nod in recognition of this feeling. Janet points out, "People, like the women in the program, can also be part of the solution, Amanda. You don't have to handle this pain all by yourself, even though you always have. You can take a chance and trust us to support you, just like you are trusting Josie right now."

Amanda begins to sit up and stops rocking. Josie has snot all over her shirt from Amanda's sobs, and doesn't notice and doesn't care. It will dry. For the moment, the crisis has been averted by the kindness of the other women. This is why chemical dependency counseling is so often a group process — it is powerful medicine.

Janet

Janet is a 53 year old, weathered, 25 year lead rehab counselor who radiates maternal energy and common sense. Grounded, with a sense of humor to help her keep perspective, she has lost a lot of clients over the years. Sometimes it's liver disease, over-dose, poisoning, cancer, or heart failure. Addiction is a lethal disease, and the urgency of death never leaves her. It spills out into her personal life and relationships, when she has them. Many of the rehab counselors she knows have a trail of damaged relationships behind them, and sometimes she wonders if temporary relationships, one client at a time, is all people like her can really handle. Addiction counselors are highly aware of lost opportunities, squandered relationships, and abandoned families. More intimacy—longer commitment—begins to feel too risky. She shudders when she thinks of her married friends because their vulnerability to loss terrifies her.

Despite this, the recovering community has kept Janet relatively sane and completely sober for 25 years, and her love and respect for the recovery process is bone-deep. Janet stopped drinking abruptly when she was in a near-fatal car accident while under the influence of alcohol. Fortunately at 2:30 am when she swerved into the other lane and slammed into the meridian, traffic was light and other drivers were able to avoid her so no one else was injured. Janet credits God with the fact that she is still alive, and recovery became her religion and longest relationship. The liturgy of the meeting (the readings, the prayers) are endlessly comforting to her in their repetitiveness. Her heart lightens as the simple openings are read, and there are so many familiar faces, even in a meeting of strangers.

As Janet re-enters her office to chart the women's group, she sees the Clinical Director chatting with a client before heading back toward the office to chart the Men's group. Janet finds herself hoping Ricardo's progress notes are current because the Clinical Director's beady eyes will quickly notice any discrepancies.

Meanwhile she types in her last note, gets a sip of coffee, and she beckons to the Intern, Sarah, to join her for Community group.

Community Group

Janet, Sarah, and Jorge (the Chemical Dependency Tech) are leading the community group this morning. This is an hour long "house meeting" that allows the residents to give each other feedback, express appreciation and concerns, and let the counselors know what might be needed for the household. The primary goal for the facilitator is to not let it become a "bitch session" where clients whine and complain about rules and weekend staff that aren't present for the meeting. Everyone goes around the circle with a one feeling word check-in then the group is opened up for concerns. There are the predictable concerns: the DVD player sticks; they want more movie choices on the weekend; and the front bathroom has a leak at the bottom of the toilet. One of the clients, Frankie, asks if it would be possible to vary their outside meetings between NA and AA since he gets more out of NA because he is a meth addict. There are nods around the room. Marla appreciates Paul for his sense of humor, and Karen appreciates the group for making her welcome. As the group breaks up, Janet is concerned that Ricardo still has not appeared.

This means Janet will be leading Ricardo's 11:30 am psycho-education group so when she returns to the office she quickly flips through the next topic in the curriculum. She takes a big bite of another donut as she realizes she will be leading a relapse prevention group and is so bored by this topic she could cry. She looks at the overly familiar lecture outline, and desperately starts flipping through the video cabinet in her head to see if there is something she can show and therapeutically justify it. Nope.

Psychoeducation Group

As she grabs her curriculum and pads into the group room Janet notices Carla sliding into the farthest chair in the room. Carla's hair is lank, unwashed and it is obvious she slept in the clothes she has not changed for two days. Carla is on Ricardo's case load and is obviously slipping through the cracks. *"Probably not hot enough,"* Janet thinks. *"Ok, that was snarky,"* she chides herself. As Janet begins the check-in she notices that Carla's eyes seem heavy and her breathing is slow. It hits Janet in the chest that Carla is loaded. She can feel her instinctive adrenalin rush of resentment—*"I hate when they bring that shit in the house,"* she thinks. *"Should I call her out on it now? I don't have any back up staff to take the group – Jorge, the CD Tech on duty, can't bottle a female,"* she mulls. She decides to test Carla later and tries to screen her out as she turns her attention to the group.

Looking at Carla gives Janet a group exercise idea.

She looks around the room at the recovering faces turned toward her. Some of them engaged, most of them lost in thought or still detoxing. Carla looks asleep. As she watches Carla, Janet remembers when she believed others couldn't see signs of her intoxication, and the general lack of self-awareness that lead to so many "light-bulb moments" once she was sober.

"Good morning! I want to spend some time with you today talking about the way we see ourselves. When we're using drugs and alcohol our view of ourselves isn't very accurate, and our decision making can be a set up for failure as a result. We can only work with the information we have." She turns to the white board and draws a box with four squares—the Johari Window.

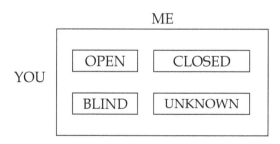

"What this means is that there are things about you that you are comfortable revealing, and the information is open to everyone. That's the open box. Can you think of an example of something about you that you and everyone else knows about you?" she asks the group.

"I'm sad about losing Joey?" Amanda asks.

"Exactly," Janet smiles.

She continues. "Then there is information that is known to you but is secret from everyone else. Can anyone think of an example?"

"If it's a secret, we couldn't say!" Paul quips. Janet laughs. "Touché. Examples of this might be jealousy you have about an ex, or dishonesty no one else knows about." Janet turns back to the white board. "Then there's information about you that everyone else can see, but you're blind to. This includes your tone of voice, level of anger, attitude you might be showing. Does this make sense?"

"You mean when my Mom says I'm "In a mood," and I have no idea what she means?" says Angie.

"Are you figuring it out the longer you are here?" Janet asks.

Angie laughs. "Jesse says the same thing to me during double-scrub, and he means I'm being irritable when he tells me what to do."

"That's a great example," Janet grins. "Finally there's the unknown box which is stuff that is unknown to you and everyone else. Examples of this include issues you may have from your childhood, or anxiety you have that you aren't aware of." Janet turns away from the white board.

"We are going to spend the next hour taking a look at what might be true for each of you in those boxes, which means you will have to give each other information to fill out your blind box. Get into pairs and start working on your Johari windows. You may have to take some emotional risks to give each other honest feedback. I'll walk around and help you, and then we'll get together and talk about what you learned."

There's the sound of screeching chairs and moving feet as the clients turn and pair up. Meanwhile, Janet sees Carla head to the bathroom (which is just as well) and Jane gestures for Jorge to follow her, since partnering with her would not be healthy for another client. Janet walks around the pairs helping everyone stay on task, and the energy of the room begins to lift.

Group turns out better than Janet expects because she has two ADHD people in the group who learn by participation, and are good at drawing the other client's into the mix. Janet loves ADHD people in general, even though they seem to irritate some of the other counselors. Most people in early recovery share the shortened attention span of an ADHD person, but don't have their energy level and search for stimulation. They learn through sharing and she would rather have to help someone with ADHD contain themselves in a group than have the detoxing, fish-eyed stare of over-medicated opiate addicts on too much suboxone. Actually, ADD/ADHD and people with Learning Disabilities are statistically over-represented in treatment and incarceration settings so sometimes they seem to outnumber the other client's in the treatment center. In fact, Janet has always thought the average NA meeting looks like an ADHD festival! Janet smiles to herself as she heads in to Clinical Staffing meeting and spies the Clinical Director on the phone. As usual he looks pissed off about something and she can hear his sharp tone as he abruptly ends his call. Ricardo has finally arrived and is checking his Facebook page.

Clinical Staffing

Ricardo

Speaking of ADD, Ricardo has been clean and sober for three years and has recently been certified as a counselor. He was motivated toward counseling by his sister who suggested that he was a good listener. Mostly he wanted to use his 15 year heroin addiction experience to help others. Other than drug dealing, Ricardo has almost no other job experience and the financial aid he got in school carried him during the first three years clean. Unfortunately, he doesn't really understand people who don't like the Twelve Step program and he finds needy people and liars irritating. He often feels his mind wandering during one-on-one's, but he really likes the teaching part because he usually has a lot to say. He doesn't seem to notice that the clients roll their eyes or doodle on their handouts because he has not learned how to fully engage them in the conversation.

Much to Janet's frustration the Clinical Director doesn't seem to be bothered by Ricardo's lack of empathy for people who don't work a Twelve Step program. This is most likely due to the fact that the Clinical Director has 35 years in NA himself. Ricardo is bilingual and good natured; he doesn't ask for help or report client issues. He rarely has client conflicts, instead waits for troubling clients to finish the program and move on. The irony is that his greatest asset – Spanish language skills - has never been used. They have never been referred a monolingual client!

Janet's eyes light up and her mood lightens when she sees Kym, the Family Counselor. Kym joined the treatment team as an Intern, and Janet was her supervisor. Kym is warm, sharp, funny, perceptive, and very competent. The families love her and clients gravitate towards her. The women's eyes lock in conspiracy as they both glance at Ricardo, and they share a quick grin.

The Clinical Director

The Clinical Director looks worn today, obviously tired and physically uncomfortable. It's most likely his liver because his first round of Hep C treatment wasn't effective. He is very old school – a 30 year rehab veteran who is quick to confront client "bullshit" and considers the new Motivational Interviewing and individualized treatment approaches "enabling" and "coddling." A graduate of Synanon himself, he is quick to feel challenged when disagreed with, and has been known to escalate with clients and throw them out of treatment for disrespect. He is also quick to look down Kym's shirt.

The sound of a Harley announces the arrival of the weekend CD Tech, Jesse, who hurries in at the last minute rustling his open Jack and the Box bag as he scoots up to the table. The CD Intern Sarah is right on his heels, and Janet finds herself wondering if they are hooking up. Janet's stomach rumbles at the smell of his fries, and tries not to watch him eat to avoid snatching the fries out of his hand! Janet loves to hear from Jesse because clients are the most real on the weekends and evenings when the counselors go home. Jesse knows the program culture and watches for client over-associations. The other CD Techs, Keisha, Jorge and Carl get seated as well. Sure enough, Jesse leads out with "I think Carla's loaded. She was nodding out in the smoking area when I came in."

The evening counselor, Eddie, arrives to hear Jesse's statement and echoes Jesse's observation.

This was a reminder to Janet that she needed to bottle Carla, so headed out to conduct a urine screen. Janet hates this part of her job – watching people pee and then dipping the test stick. She calls to Carla outside and asks her to come in and test. Carla rises from the chair slowly, a little unsteady on her feet. As she comes in and they head up the hall, Janet asks her,

"I notice you seem to be having hard time staying awake today. Is there anything you want to tell me about the test you are about to take?"

"Nope," Carla mutters as she dutifully drops her pants and positions the urine cup. Carla has a hard time hitting the cup, though manages to catch enough of the urine for Janet to conduct the test. Carla and Janet wash their hands as they wait for the single or double stripe indicator. Sure enough it tests positive for opiates.

"Okay Carla," Janet says as she gently steers her out of the bathroom. "I'm going to have you lay down in the detox area for now and talk to the staff about our next move." Carla doesn't protest, and seems relieved to just fade out on the bed.

Janet returns to the case meeting saying, "Okay, Jesse's right. Carla's loaded. Ricardo, she's yours so how do you want to handle this?"

Ricardo looks slightly puzzled as he turns to the Clinical Director, "Well, we have to kick her out don't we? I guess I have to go tell her to pack up and call someone to come and get her."

"Carla doesn't have anyone to come and get her," Kym says.

"She doesn't have any family so we need to try to send her to the women's detox if she is willing to go."

"I want to know how the hell she's loaded in a residential rehab!" the Clinical Director blurts. This is obviously an important question because it raises the concern that there are other clients either using or who have been put at risk by her using. Did she use all the drugs she had or are there more?

"Ricardo and I will handle having her pack up and arranging for transport to the women's detox," Janet offers.

Predictably, the Clinical Director takes the presence of drugs in the facility personally. His face begins to redden as he barks to Jorge to follow him and do a room search. "This shit can't happen in my house!" he rails, on the lookout for someone to blame. Janet knows the abruptness of his approach will create fall out that she will spend the rest of the day cleaning up during process groups. It's not the first time she's shared his frustration, yet she dreads the collateral damage his ham-fisted approach always causes.

The real culprit is understaffing. Leaving only two CD techs per shift on the weekend and evenings creates a giant hole in the safety net that residential rehab is supposed to provide. Managing 15 people in early recovery is like herding cats!

Everyone is operating from their limbic system, which means they are dominated by emotion. Their frontal lobe logic and impulse control has not fully recovered, so you have a room full of impulsive people with limited judgment. The staff has to function as external logic and frontal lobes at this early juncture, and understaffing make this almost impossible. Instead the clients consult with each other – receiving the same bad advice they would give. This is a recipe for disaster.

Eventually the room searches are complete and everyone has been drug tested and proven clean. Carla states that she took the last two oxycontin's she had smuggled in, and there does not appear to be any other drugs on the premises.

Janet is going to have to address the house silence as everyone colluded for the last two days in Carla's using. Fear of "snitching" runs deep for the clients, especially the criminal justice clients. Helping to reframe telling as a way to create house safety is an ongoing challenge.

The team reassembles for the Clinical Staffing meeting with only a few minutes left before Janet's afternoon process group. The counselors triage their cases to address the more urgent clients and decide to start with the remaining clients at the next meeting. The Clinical Director is still looking stormy as he grabs his coffee mug and takes his seat. Ricardo leads off with a concern about Mark, who is due to complete the program next week.

"I was looking through Mark's paperwork and I realized he has a 290 (sex offender) charge, so we can't transfer him to the SLE (Sober Living Home) next week when he completes. What do we do with these guys?"

In the treatment center county, the county District Attorney's office has a good neighbor agreement that licensed and certified addiction treatment centers and sober living homes will not house sex offenders. This is an attempt to address the "not in my backyard" problem all treatment centers face. However, prison overcrowding dictates an increased number of early releases and included in this population are sex offenders.

Janet's face reflects her frustration. What really annoys her about this situation is that murderers and extortionists can live in the neighborhood, even meth lab operators. However, if you get a 290 for peeing in public or having sex with a minor when you are 18 years old you are automatically disqualified from housing. It is the only charge that requires lifelong check-in's regardless of the circumstances. The guy who has sex with a minor at 18 is classified the same as serial rapists and child molesters.

Jane resists getting on her familiar soap box due to lack of time and suggests that Ricardo check out the unlicensed homes. "After all, we want to make sure these guys are placed in the LEAST supervised homes possible, right?" she quips.

"Does he have any family?" Kym asks. "No one has come for family day, but that doesn't mean there isn't someone he could stay with."

"I think parole has to approve his placement if there is," the Clinical Director adds. "You need to talk to Mark and find out because we only have a week to solve this problem, and parole needs to make a site visit. Otherwise grab the list Janet mentioned and have him start calling. Why the hell are we waiting 'til the last minute like this anyway?" he addresses Ricardo pointedly.

Ricardo has trouble making eye contact with the Clinical Director, and makes his usual excuses about paperwork burdens while Eddie jumps in to rescue him.

"I am worried about Marla. When I watch her in group it's like the lights are on and no-one's home. Has anyone else noticed that?" Eddie asks.

"I noticed it last weekend," Kym says. "She seemed okay when I was talking to her, but when Jesse came in and asked her a question it looked like she left her body. She was really slow to answer him."

"That's exactly what I mean," Eddie says. "I can't tell if she's listening, checked-out, or maybe even on something."

"Well the house was just tested," Jorge offers, "Everyone's clean."

"I'm due to have a one-on-one with her today," Janet observes, "Let me see where she's at. She's only been here a week or so, so I don't have a good handle on her yet."

Kym has been thinking, "You know, I watched her with her husband last weekend and I remember that she didn't say very much. Of course, the guy is so wired he takes up most of the oxygen in the room!" she laughs.

Jesse smiles and nods, "I know what you're saying. Normally greeting the families is no big deal. I check their bags, ask them to sign in, bada bing. But this guy has to argue with me about why I am checking his bag for Marla, wonders who sees the sign in sheet later, and gets all pissy when I tell him he has to leave the diet soda 12-pack in the car because we don't allow caffeine."

"How did the other families respond to him?" Janet asks.

"The other families watched him but didn't chime in," Kym answers. "I was watching Marla though, and she had no expression on her face, she looked flat."

"It's not the first time she's seen him take over a room," Janet comments. "My guess is she's learned to just give him room."

"She looks like she's disappearing. Actually..." Kym mulls. "I think the lady has been traumatized, definitely by him but I wonder if it goes back before the marriage."

"You mean like her childhood?" Sarah the Intern asks.

"That's exactly what I mean, Sarah," Kym smiles at her.

"I'll check it out later when I meet with her," Janet says. "If it is trauma, then we'll need to hook her up for longer term therapy with a trauma counselor."

"Just make sure they understand addicts," Eddie interrupts. "Otherwise they'll probably slap her on some bullshit medicine and she'll get ANOTHER addiction." Eddie's comment reflects a common sentiment among addition counselors who tend to be leery of mental health professionals. Many addiction counselors were seeing therapists while abusing their drug of choice, so they know from personal experience how poorly the mental health professional identifies and treats addicts. This is mostly due to the long standing belief in mental health that the addiction is a symptom of the larger underlying problem, like depression. So if you treat the depression, the drinking will stop. At least that's how the logic goes. However addiction is an illness in its own right, and the individual will more likely have a dual diagnosis, both depression and addiction. If both disorders are not treated they will trigger relapse with each other.

Janet nods in agreement and realizes that she will need to slip out of the room and do the process group. As she leaves, she notices Ricardo texting under the conference table. *"I swear he looks like he's masturbating,"* she thinks.

Kym knows she's going to have to address the drug use in Family group, as the clients begin to report to their families. Families are quick to blame the treatment program for the break in security, and it will be Kym's job to continue to educate the families about the disease of addiction. The craving of addiction feels like a survival need – a survival need that can overpower the need for sleep, food and sex. The neurochemistry of addiction (the power of craving) is confusing to families because using seems like a choice. And it is, initially. Kym is particularly worried about the Flynn family.

This is Frankie's third treatment program in five years. Frankie's parents look haunted and heavy as they relate the financial devastation and involvement in the criminal justice system that has come with Frankie's addiction. Frankie's Mom, Katherine, weeps as she recalls their relationship before he first discovered pot, then cocaine, and then crack. Frankie has seizures sometimes when he uses crack, yet this doesn't seem to stop him. Frankie's parents startle when the phone rings at night, terrified it's the police or even worse, the morgue. Actually, Frankie's Dad, Bill, is relieved when it's the police because at least Frankie is safe and they know where he will be for the time being instead of picturing him wandering homeless and vulnerable. Frankie can't live with his parents when he discharges because the last time he was out he stole his grandmother's jewelry. Bill made the rounds and hit all the local pawn shops, eventually able to buy some of it back. Frankie's sister Jackie is furious with him. She is tired of ruined holidays and broken promises. She has told her parents that if they let Frankie live with them again she will no longer visit their home.

Kym is worried because Katherine's health has deteriorated markedly over the last five years. She has developed high blood pressure, colitis, and now suffers from migraines. Bill is furious at Frankie for making Katherine ill, and Bill is terrified of losing her. Kym can feel his eyes fill with pleading as he hopes she will give them a solution to Frankie's illness and heal their family. Kym knows from taking a brief family history that Katherine comes from a family of alcoholics, and her fear of lost relationships and anxiety did not begin with Frankie's addiction. In fact, Kym has observed Frankie behave in a parentified way with his mother, careful to shield her from emotional honesty that he thinks she will not be able to handle. The longer he's clean, the more she seems to want to insinuate herself in all aspects of his life, and Kym suspects part of Frankie's original drug use may have been a way to create a separation between him and his mom – creating an invisible wall between them to give him some ability to move forward in the world without her. Unfortunately, he's genetically wired for addiction, so what began as an attempt at solution quickly morphed into a problem. Kym knows the family will flip out Saturday when they hear about drug use in the facility, and she will need to do damage control.

Process Group

As the client's settled in, Janet could feel their restlessness. They had no doubt been affected by Carla's using, and possibly more so by carrying her secret. When there's a secret in a recovery center, the clients quickly become uneasy. They will get restless and even act out under the pressure. Janet decides to address Carla's use head-on.

"Okay guys, I think it makes sense to start by talking about Carla. You all know she's loaded, been loaded since family group most likely. We're going to send her for detox, so she'll be fine. My main concern at this point is how you're affected. What kind of things came up for you when you saw she was loaded… and didn't say anything?" Janet opened.

"I thought she was sleepy at first, so I didn't really catch on until I saw her nodding during the Narcotics Anonymous Meeting Saturday night," Kevin offers.

"When you caught on, what did you feel?" Janet asks.

"Honestly? I wondered if she had more pills, but I was too chicken to ask her," he admitted.

"Did anyone else feel triggered to use?" Janet asks the group.

Josie raises her hand, and so does Amanda.

"Why do you think you didn't say anything to make the house safer for you?"

"Because I've been there, and I didn't want to embarrass her or get her in trouble," Josie answers.

"I get that thinking. I've had that thinking," Janet agrees. "And part of recovery is changing the way we take care of ourselves. When you let yourself stay in uncomfortable or unsafe situations for too long, it becomes natural to think of using again. One of the things I know you hear us say a lot is hanging out with people who use is really slippery."

"Carl says if you hang around the barbershop, you will get a haircut," Paul laughs.

"Exactly!" Janet smiles. "It's part of treating yourself like you matter to be more protective of your healing. You DESERVE support in your early recovery, not unnecessary struggle. I want the treatment center to be a safe place for you, a place of healing."

Everyone nods.

"Okay, I get that we should have said something. But why did the Clinical Director have to be such a dick about it? I felt like I was being interrogated!" Paul comments.

Janet nods. "I know he can be heavy handed at times. He takes what we do here very personally, and feels responsible for the safety of the house."

"I think he was disappointed when he didn't catch us!" Mike laughs.

"Maybe," Janet smiles, "it's important for him to feel like the situation is stable."

"Anything else going on with you?" Janet says as she shifts the conversation and begins the check-in.

Marla

After process group Janet asks Marla if she can meet with her for a one-on-one. They settle into Janet's office area for some privacy.

"Marla, we were talking in Clinical Staffing, and several of the counselors noted that sometimes in group you appear to be preoccupied, like you're somewhere else. I especially notice it when emotions start getting heated. Have you noticed this?" Janet asks.

Marla thinks. "I've always been teased about being a space cadet, if that's what you mean. I lose track of the conversation sometimes."

"Have you always done this, or is it since you've been drinking?"

"No, I remember doing it as a kid, usually during family visits or during holidays."

"What was happening during those times?"

"Well, my step-dad would drink a lot and get a little out of hand."

"What did 'out of hand' look like?" Janet probed.

"Oh, you know. Hitting, yelling. One time he pulled a knife on my mom," she says with no emotion.

"That sounds terrifying!" Janet comments.

Marla shrugs.

"Was there anyone there to comfort you?" Janet asks.

"Sometimes my grandfather was there. But he would stumble in my bedroom sometimes after drinking with my step-dad." Marla continues, expressionless. She looks like she's beginning to leave her body.

Janet touches Marla's arm briefly to bring her back. "Marla, did you learn to go away from your body to cope with these things?"

"Sometimes I would feel like I was floating up to the ceiling. Is that what you mean?"

Janet smiles. "Yes, it is. That was a smart thing to do, and it allowed you to survive a horrible experience. The problem is now that you're safe, you still get triggered to leave your body – it's not always in your control. This can leave you pretty vulnerable."

Marla sits quietly.

"Have you ever noticed that drinking makes you feel the same way?"

Marla nods. "Do you think this is why I drink?" Marla asks.

"I think you drink because you're an alcoholic, Marla. But I suspect you started drinking because of depression, anxiety and trauma connected to your childhood, so we will have to help you manage your floating feelings if you are going to stay sober. Are you willing to let me find an outside professional to help you?" Janet asks.

"If you think it will help me, I'll try it." Marla agrees.

Janet

When Janet returns from group and her one-on-one with Marla, she glances at the clock and realizes that she has her own therapy appointment in 45 minutes. She charts both group and the session with Marla and heads out before she is caught in traffic. Janet feels strongly that therapy is vital to her mental health, she knows being surrounded by the active disease of addiction can trigger her. She's particularly anxious today because she notices she's chatting a lot with a new resident, Paul. She is finding herself looking forward to seeing him when she comes in every day, and can always find time to meet with him even if it puts her behind on her paperwork or makes her run late to group. As much as she can see this is happening, she feels compelled to see him and realizes she feels more alive right now than she has in a long time. This is very dangerous to her license and his recovery, so she has been careful not to share her feelings with

Paul directly. However she knows he can sense her availability and this scares her, as well as violates everything she has stood for over the years as a professional.

"I feel like I'm losing my mind," she tells her therapist. "I don't know what's wrong with me. I've never acted like this before. The other day I found myself looking online to see if people with felonies can get passports when I was buying my ticket for my trip to the conference in Canada! What the hell?"

"Janet, tell me about the way he treats you. What's happening when he talks to you?"

"When he looks at me it's as though there is no one else in the room. He remembers what I say to him, and he makes me laugh. He tells me stories about his life, chaotic crazy stories, and I find myself listening as long as he will keep talking. I am endlessly entertained. Honestly, I catch myself finding reasons to touch him, and I think I want to do him." She can't look her therapist in the eye as she says this.

"I haven't felt this way in over two years—since David left me for the mouth-breather skank. You know, I heard he knocked her up, and God forgive me, I keep hoping she'll die in childbirth. I hate her so much!" Janet can feel the tears behind her eyes.

"Why do you make it all about her?" the therapist asks, "David made the decision to lie to you, to hook up with her?"

"I know. I don't know. I hate her because I can picture him saying the same things to her he said to me, the attention he is giving her that he used to give me. She's such a dumbshit – how could he choose a bimbo like that when I would have done anything for him? I DID do anything for him!" The tears are falling in force now, and Janet grabs for a Kleenex.

"Maybe that's the problem?" the therapist inserts.

Janet doesn't answer—remembering the hours spent working on his thesis or working extra shifts so he could study.

"So, this client, Paul, helps you remember the way it felt when things were good?"

"Yeah. I guess that's it." Janet blows her nose. "The truth is I guess it's not about Paul at all. I've been so shut down since David left. You remember... I wore the same clothes every day, barely managed to walk through my day. Even though I am functioning way better on the outside, I think Paul has stirred up the part of me that has been numbed out."

"In some ways it is more painful to remember when I was happy, when I was content just being in David's presence, smelling him, kissing him simply out of joy because I loved his sweet face so much. I wasn't enough ... it's not the first time that I wasn't chosen..." Janet sounds desolate as she recalls how sterile her world has been without him.

Her world has been sterile before. An adult child of two alcoholic parents, Janet learned very early in life that she was on her own. While her parents were able to provide the basics (food-clothing-shelter) there was little availability for comforting or participation in her life. She remembers coming home from school and going straight to her room, passing her mother asleep on the couch. Her father was in technical sales and very frequently overseas, so it was Janet and her mom most of the time. Janet remembers looking at her mother and realizing that Janet felt older than her child-mom. It was natural for Janet to make most of the decisions and keep the household organized. She tried not to "bother" her depressed, inebriated mom who was obviously suffering in her own isolation and loneliness. When her dad was home he would attempt to "take control" which usually consisted of barking orders and making irritated and critical observations. As much as she longed for someone to be the parent so she could just do her life, having her father step in was worse. The house seemed to breathe when he would leave for his next extended trip.

Unfortunately, she's had a series of relationships with men just like her father. Seduced by their apparent decisiveness and confidence, it soon becomes obvious that they have very few coping skills and even less emotional availability. The anxiety and fear of risk taking below their surface strength usually engages Janet in caretaking and eventually she assumes control of their lives much like she did growing up. This pattern is so normal for her that she has a difficult time respecting the men around her, noticing and judging their hesitation and passivity. She has even been known to say, "If I could find a man with bigger balls than me I would marry him." It has never occurred to her that in a healthy relationship you share power. In her world, only one person has it and she is so fatigued at this point in her life she thinks she would like to surrender the power and just "have someone take care of me." Needlessly to say she has never been close to a relationship where this might happen, so she trudges through life believing that Noah forgot to put two of her on the ark.

Eventually the therapy winds up for the hour, Janet feeling more clear about the intensity of her reaction to Paul and how little it really has to do with him. She feels more in control when she thinks about returning to work the next day and has a stab of gratitude that she has the support system she has. It helps that Duck Dynasty is on and she has the rest of the Oreo bag left.

TUESDAY

The next morning Janet arrives at the center just as the Correctional Van pulls into the driveway. They are delivering two men from state prison who have qualified for the new community placement program. This allows them to complete the last 6 months of their sentence in a rehabilitation center. They arrive in the van shackled and wearing paper jumpsuits. She watches as the ankle cuffs are removed and they are handed their paper bags with the possessions they had when they were arrested. They are delivered to the building and Jorge signs for them, like UPS parcels, and their custody shifts to the treatment center. The men enter the building and then change into the clothes stored in their bags. They need to contact family to bring clothes and toiletries to the center and if there was no family, then Jorge will issue them packets of underwear and socks and the guys can choose clothes from the donation closet.

After changing, the men come out into the main client area, warily checking their surroundings and getting their bearings as they meet the other residents. As Janet watches them she is reminded of the last time she introduced a new kitten to the two older cats. They sniffed each other, circled each other and quickly established each one's place in the pecking order. A senior resident takes them on a tour of the facility and shows them where they will be sleeping. Janet will meet with one man, and Ricardo the other, to orient them and complete the intake process.

The clients are meeting with the yoga and meditation facilitator, so Janet ushers her new client, Raul, into her office to begin the intake process. She watches him assessing her, adjusting his behavior by what he thinks he's seeing and what he thinks she wants to hear. She would love to ask him what he sees, but that would be confrontational straight out of the gate. She can tell he is program savvy by his answers to the questions she is asking him, and he is very deliberate in his word choice. He wants to look open enough to be "trusted" yet keep his cards close to his vest. Janet never reads a history before meeting with new clients in order to form her own initial impression, but the term institutionalized floats up as she watches him, and she wonders if he has been traumatized doing state time. More and more state penitentiary men and women are being early released due to severe overcrowding. With them comes an increase in Post Incarceration Syndrome (PICS), which is a cluster of symptoms including institutionalized behavior, Post Traumatic Stress, Antisocial personality traits, and Social Sensory Deficit syndrome resulting from prolonged periods in solitary confinement.

Raul is 34 years old, and has spent a total of three years of the last 20 out of custody. The youngest child of a large, sprawling Mexican family still living in Fresno, he was introduced to gang life and methamphetamine early by his older brothers. Raul is bright, artistic, and uneducated due to leaving school at 15 years old to work with the family business and run with his brothers at night. During his time out in the community he managed to have two children with two separate women, and he has never met either child. Now that he's back out, he is hoping to reunite with his youngest child's mother and meet his son. He always wanted a son.

His expression is flat and hard to read - an expression honed in incarceration as an important survival skill. He managed incarceration well, having moved up the ranks in prison gang affiliation so he is treated with respect by inmates who are aware of him. It is likely the respect will extend to the treatment community as well, as many of the other residents are familiar with the gang structure if not with him personally. He's what Janet thinks of as a "shot caller," and forming an alliance with him will be crucial to maintain community stability.

Janet finds state guys like Raul hard to work with because prison culture has taught him to be indirect with his intentions and say what he needs to say to accomplish his agenda. And there is always an agenda for everything he says or every request he makes. Conning is like breathing to Raul, and Janet finds herself dreading the inevitable boundary pushing that comes with a person with no respect for other people or the rules they live by. Sometimes the arrogance and entitlement of the convict's disregard for the house structure makes her want to scream, and there are days when she has to call her sponsor at lunch and vent so she won't go off on one of them in group. She reminds herself that everyone deserves a chance to recover and to keep her focus even if his intentions are dishonest. The Department of Corrections is the most common interventionist with addicts and alcoholics, and being arrested has saved the lives of many of the people she has worked with. She reminds herself that the goal is to introduce Raul to recovery as an option, and he will make the decision for himself. Janet wonders how Ricardo is doing.

As Janet facilitates the Community group with Jorge, Ricardo sits across from Angel and recognizes a kindred spirit. Unlike Janet, Ricardo has a tendency to talk a lot about himself and his story, much like a sponsor, having tuned out the lecture on appropriate self-disclosure in school. He is convinced sharing his experience will create a bond with the clients, and they will trust him because if he can do it, they can do it. He hopes to be an inspiration to them.

Ricardo discovers that 28 year old Angel also used heroin after finding opiate pills like Vicodin too expensive on the street. Heroin is much cheaper, so he switched over. This is Angel's first time in drug and alcohol treatment although he has a 10 year alcohol and drug use history. He has never thought of himself as addicted since he didn't use when he was locked up even when the other guys did. Then again, he didn't have anyone to put money on his books, and the money he earned from his prison jobs barely helped him get the basics at the commissary. His parents are local and he has not spoken to his dad in many years. He is too embarrassed about the mess he has made of his life. Ricardo asks him if he thinks his drug use may be the reason his life has gone so badly, and Angel ponders this. He is at least open to the idea, though has a lot to learn. Angel will benefit tremendously from treatment due to his openness, and he has no preconceived ideas because this is his first time through. Ricardo feels a stir of enthusiasm as he has Angel sign the intake paperwork.

The men have finished processing in time for Ricardo's 11:30 psychoeducation group, and he is looking forward to making a good impression on the new guys. The new intern, Sarah, is sitting in to observe because she is not yet ready to co-facilitate the group. Ricardo finds himself preening a little as she looks at him expectantly. Chemical Dependency interns are always a breath of fresh air to a treatment center. They tend to be eager, open, curious and willing to get involved. The downside is they notice all the irregularities and ethics violations because they are studying them in school. Ricardo likes them because they look up to him, at least initially.

Janet can hear Ricardo's opening monologue (as she calls it) through the wall as she hammers out her paperwork. Her heart goes out to Sarah, and she hopes that Sarah has a good bullshit detector. Most addicts and alcoholics do. The client's certainly do, and they find Ricardo particularly easy to read. If they reflect back the image of Ricardo's values, their stay in the center will be pretty easy. He's too afraid of being disliked to challenge them, and most of them know this. They know that sharing a cigarette with him in the smoking area, and swapping war stories is the smartest thing they can do to keep him engaged and non-confrontational.

Unfortunately, Ricardo's desire to be liked means he rarely enforces treatment center structure, which makes more work for the rest of the staff. When Janet responds to program infractions she can anticipate that Ricardo's clients will complain to him later, claiming that she doesn't understand them as well as he does, and they will ask him to run interference. Fortunately the Clinical Director is an even harder-ass than Janet, so Ricardo quickly learns this won't work.

Laura

Janet noticed that Laura looked preoccupied in women's group yesterday morning, and makes a point of asking her to come in and talk later that afternoon. Laura is a beautiful young woman who became addicted to amphetamines to lose weight. Laura was prescribed appetite suppressants when she was becoming the largest girl in the class at the age of twelve. She began to develop early and was acutely conscious that her breasts were larger than the other girls'. Even as an adult she tends to wear oversized sweaters and baggy skirts and jeans no matter what her body weight might be. She entered treatment very thin, even gaunt, and the regular meal times have caused her to begin to fill out the extra ten pounds she needed to look healthy. However, Janet recognized Laura's spaciness in group and pale complexion as potential signs of purging. Janet gently pointed out what she was seeing, and asked her about purging her meals. Laura looked ashamed as she first denied, then admitted that during family group last week her mother pointed out that Laura's cheeks looked full. What Laura heard her mother say was, "You look like a disgusting chipmunk, you fat ass. You look terrible," which started the purging cycle. In fact, Laura's mother had noticed her filling out and mentioned it as a positive sign of health. Laura's distortion around food and body weight meant that even the simplest of comments could be interpreted as a harsh rebuke.

Janet and Laura altered Laura's treatment plan to address the purging, and Janet put in a call to a local therapist who specializes in eating disorders to see if she was taking new patients. In the meantime, Janet requested that Laura remain in the dining area at least 30 minutes after her meal and not go to the bathroom. Janet and Laura identified a female client that Laura feels safe with to keep her company during that half hour, which gives Laura practice in using outside support. Laura requested a hug as she started to leave the session, which Janet gave, and then Janet sat down to chart the session.

As Janet was finishing the last of her chart note there was a knock at the door, and there stood Kevin in the doorway. Janet wanted to heave a deep sigh. Kevin is a 22 year old prescription medication addict who is constantly pill seeking. He is always asking for an aspirin, a Unison to sleep, Benadryl for his allergies… he somatizes every feeling he has so is constantly on the alert for any physical ache or pain. Talking to Kevin is like talking to a health and procedure obsessed 70 year old, and Janet tries to hide her irritation.

"Janet," Kevin begins, "I have this really weird feeling in my chest, and one of the clients told me that you can seizure between 3-6 days after you stop drinking because your blood pressure shoots up. How will I know I am going to have a seizure? Is there a warning first?"

"Do you have a history of seizures, Kevin?" Janet asked.

"Well, no. But my grandfather had a heart attack, and I have only been clean a week. Should I worry?"

"Honestly Kevin I suspect you are just fine. You are not an alcoholic and you are on detox medicine for your opiate withdrawal to manage your symptoms."

"I know you're probably right. But I'm wondering if I should take an aspirin just in case. I think that doctors have people take an aspirin to thin their blood when they are worried about heart disease."

"You know Kevin, I don't think we need to take that precaution. I do want you to notice that your first response to anxiety is to think about taking pills. We have a lot of other stress reducing choices like meditation, listening to music, exercise, even taking a walk out back. I really encourage you to practice other types of things to help you manage your emotions while you're here."

Janet could see the hesitation in his face as he nodded in agreement and wandered off to his room. Janet makes a note in his chart to speak with Kym about Kevin's family situation and his support system.

Sarah

Janet notes that it is time to meet with her intern, Sarah. She's curious to hear the young woman's impression of the center as she starts to apply what she's been learning in class. Sarah appeared promptly for supervision, which Janet is careful to appreciate. So many new counselors come to the field without work ethics or professionalism, and it's a treat to see Sarah show up appropriately dressed, well spoken and punctual. This is no doubt because she worked in HR before her alcoholism took over her life. Janet admires Sarah's pre-addiction skill set which makes it so much easier to pick up the pieces. When people have chaotic lives in their addiction, or start using very early there are no adult skills to "return to" in sobriety. You are learning life skills at the same time as recovery skills. Sarah's transition into the counseling field will be much smoother than Ricardo's. Ricardo was fired from his first Internship placement for bringing contraband into the treatment facility because he "felt sorry" for the guys that reminded him of himself when he was first getting clean.

Sarah is a 25 year old alcohol and drug counselor intern. She is the daughter of an alcoholic mother who has been sober 10 years through Alcoholics Anonymous. Sarah's dad is an engineer who had difficulty seeing or acknowledging his wife's drinking, largely because Sarah's mom hid it from him by drinking more during the day when he was at work. Once in a while she would be obviously drunk but this was rare.

Sarah was a freshman in high school when her mother entered AA, so Sara went to meetings with her and became familiar with the recovery culture. She loved how much happier her mom became. Eventually her mom pushed her to go to Alanon, and she has been part of the Alanon program ever since. Three years ago Sarah began to notice that her social drinking was developing a binge pattern. After a couple of nasty alcohol-fueled fights with her boyfriend, her Alanon sponsor suggested that she try AA and she now attends both AA and Alanon weekly. She is currently working her steps with her AA sponsor, and sometimes feels a little like an imposter because she stopped drinking before she had serious consequences. This is especially true when she hears horror stories from the clients. She is in transition from her work in Human Resources to the chemical dependency field because she feels strongly that this is where she belongs. This transition is made possible by her recent marriage, so she can manage the reduction in pay. Her husband is a "normie" but supports her passion for recovery, and even goes to meetings with her on occasion.

Janet worries about Sarah's tendency towards over-responsibility and sends Sarah off with some recommended reading, Phillip Beebe's 'The Codependent Counselor.' Janet assures her they will discuss the book next week. Janet suddenly feels sad as Sarah leaves as she realizes she is heading home to the cats for another Law and Order marathon. She thinks back to her conversation with her therapist the previous day, and realizes she had done a much better job with Paul today. She had chatted with him only in group settings and didn't touch him at all. Being back in touch with her actual grief for David had created perspective, even though it still shocks her that two years out of the relationship she is still so hurt; and enraged. Picturing a stop sign, she shifts her thoughts quickly before she heads down that rabbit hole. She remembers a 6 pm women's group she can catch on her way home for that extra shot of estrogen and hugs she could feel she needs before heading home and falling asleep with the latest Irvin Yalom book.

WEDNESDAY

Carolyn

When Janet arrives the next morning she reads in the log that Carolyn has been re-admitted, and realizes that Carolyn is not in the dining area for breakfast or mediation when she goes to speak with her. Concerned, she heads up the hall to Carolyn's room and can see from the doorway she is still in bed. This is Carolyn's second time in treatment having maintained sobriety about a month after discharge last time. Carolyn is a 35 year old suburban mother of two, who picked up a DUI on the way home after school with her children in the minivan. The officer allowed her to call her husband to pick up the children before taking her down to the station and booking her. Her furious husband called an attorney and bailed her out.

The first time in treatment Carolyn was defiant and angry, and determined to fight the DUI down to a wet reckless - convinced that treatment was "overkill." She had entered treatment on her attorney's advice and she spent most of her time hogging the phone during phone time to micromanage the children and household in her absence. Carolyn was mortified to be in treatment with prisoners and needle-using addicts, and listened to their stories for their differences rather than their similarities. Carolyn's children were clearly uncomfortable during family visits, mostly due to Carolyn's anger as she recited her list of grievances due to the incompetence of the treatment program staff. Kym had allowed the children to bring the family dog more for the children's sake than Carolyn's.

Given Carolyn's consistent and obvious judgment of the other clients, she had made very few friends in the program other than a couple of other chronic complainer clients. It was a very long 30 days for everyone, and the staff heaved a sigh of relief when she got her completion certificate and checked out.

A month after discharge the Clinical Director receives a call from Carolyn's husband who'd been called from a local restaurant after

Carolyn passed out in the dining area. She's been "sneaking" wine during the day, and chose that afternoon to treat herself with a wine and salad before picking up the children. On the way to the bathroom in the restaurant she trips and falls into the corner of a table and gashes her head. The paramedics are called, and she is okay though unable to drive. Her husband calls a neighbor to pick up the children, and he is on his way to pick up his wife. He asks the Clinical Director if he can bring Carolyn directly to the treatment center from the restaurant because he is unwilling to have her return home until she "gets her shit together.' Given her husband's position, and her shame at falling, Carolyn agrees to re-enter treatment. She is too intoxicated to do a full intake, so she has been put to bed until the next morning when Janet comes in.

Janet's aware that Carolyn may be overwhelmed by feelings ranging from remorse to humiliation to resentment. She quietly moves closer to Carolyn's bed to wake her, and Carolyn slowly opens her eyes and focuses. When she recognizes Janet, she turns her face to the wall. Janet pulls up a chair and asks Carolyn if she can have her "paw." Janet wants to check Carolyn's pulse and check for tremors. She has found it helpful over the years to use animal analogies to take the sting out of what she might be saying. Carolyn rolls over and compliantly holds out her arm. Carolyn's tremors are mild, which was what Janet expected. She isn't sure how much Carolyn has been drinking since she has been sneaking, so isn't sure if she needs to be on medical detox. Janet decides to call the on-call nurse to come in and take a look at her later this morning.

"Carolyn, can you tell me how you are feeling this morning?"

"I feel like shit. What do you think I'm feeling?"

"I don't know. You could be feeling a lot of things. I imagine you would also have feelings about being back here."

"My husband said I couldn't come home – he's taking the children away from me." Carolyn's voice was flat and hopeless.

"Carolyn, it's true he was pretty pissed off when he brought you.

He also called this morning because he's worried. I think there may be more to work with than you might be afraid there is."

"Our marriage has been crappy for a long time. It really got bad after my last daughter was born. I was so tired all the time... I never had energy for him when came home. I felt like I was going to come out my skin every day. I kept thinking there was something wrong with me because I was having a harder time bonding with this child than the first one. Maybe they would all be better off without me and have a chance to have a good mother if Frank remarries."

Concerned, Janet asked, "Carolyn, have you been thinking about ending your life?"

"Well, I don't have a plan, if that's what you're asking. I couldn't do that to my kids on purpose. But honestly, when my friend Joyce told me she had cancer I felt a little jealous."

"Carolyn, I think we may have missed the depression the first time you were here because you were using anger to cover it up. I think we need to have you meet with our psychiatrist and get an evaluation. If you are depressed, even have postpartum depression, you will not stay sober without help. I think helping your husband to understand this may even create a bridge for you to talk to him. What do you think?"

Carolyn was quiet for a few minutes while Janet sat patiently waiting. "I guess it's worth a shot. I knew something was wrong with me, but I couldn't admit it before. I didn't want Frank to think I was a bad mother."

Janet resists pointing out the obvious fact that driving your kids around while loaded is not good mommy behavior either.

As Carolyn gets up to get dressed for women's group, Janet heads back to the office to make a chart note and check her messages.

"How did it go?' Ricardo asked Janet when he returned from the Community group he led with the CD Tech, Keisha. Carolyn targeted him a lot when she was in treatment last time, so Ricardo is concerned to hear she has been readmitted.

"It went way better than I thought it might. She copped to depression, so I think we might actually help her this time. Kym has some serious work to do with Carolyn's husband."

"Are you going to keep her?" he asks.

"Absolutely, big guy. I wouldn't do that to you." Janet smiles.

Janet looks up as Raul opens the door without knocking. Her irritation showing, Janet asks him what he needs, and reminds him that he needs to knock before coming in because she could be in session.

"Yea, that's right. Sorry." Raul replies. "I was hoping you would call my baby's momma and ask her if she would bring my son to family day so I could meet him."

"Haven't you asked her yourself?"

"Well, she don't answer her phone and I think she might be dodging me. Maybe if you call she'd pick up."

"Raul, maybe you should respect her wishes if she doesn't want to see you?"

Raul flared, "Yeah, well that's MY baby and I have rights! That lazy bitch has no right to disrespect me and keep my baby from me!"

Janet blinked and stood still. Ricardo looked frozen.

"Raul, I get it that you haven't seen your son because you were away. I can understand why you want her to bring him here. There are also limits in what we can make people do. Do you have her address?"

"Yeah, it's in my phone in the drawer."

"Okay. After group I'll get your phone and we'll get her address. We can sit down and I will write a letter to her with you and we'll invite her to family day."

"I don't write good."

"That's why I am going to help you," Janet assures him.

"Okay," he mutters as he leaves.

Janet and Ricardo take a deep breath.

"Okay, that was intense," Ricardo quipped.

Janet just nods, and makes a note in Raul's chart. She realizes that she didn't feel threatened, just startled by his intensity. He has been able to bully his way around his entire life. It must be strange for him to lose power – probably scary too. Janet makes a mental note to ask him about this when they write his letter. She's also aware that she had felt responsible to protect Ricardo – just like she felt the need to protect her mom. *"There's a thought for therapy,"* she tells herself.

It's Janet's turn to lead the 11:30 am Psychoeducation group, so she grabs the curriculum to see what she's going to talk about. She grins as she realizes that she's going to be teaching about boundaries – internal and external boundaries. This couldn't be better timing for Raul.

Psychoeducation

"Good morning" she opens, smiling at the circle. It is interesting to her to see who pairs and cliques up in a treatment center. People connect that would normally never associate in the real world due to socioeconomic status or drug of choice. She notices that Carolyn chose to sit next to Angel, Ricardo's new client which makes her smile more broadly.

"Who knows what I mean when I say boundaries?" she asks as she writes the word on the board.

There was a brief silence until people started offering; "A fence," "A line to keep people out," etc. The class moved forward very smoothly and even Raul stopped posturing and became engaged despite himself.

"We have two types of boundaries, and they exist for **Protection** — to keep people out and **Containment** — to keep us in!

Janet turns to the board and writes,

<u>External</u>: These are our outer boundaries – our bodies, our possessions, and our physical space. In American culture this is about an arm's length. So, I get to **Protect** my body and things from unwanted touching or use, and I get to **Contain** myself from touching other people or their things without their permission.

<u>Internal</u>: This is the boundary around our thoughts, feelings and reality. I can recognize that my thoughts and feelings are separate from yours. I can **Protect** my internal world from being shamed or controlled by you, and I can **Contain** myself from trying to change or control your internal world."

As Janet was leading the group she was reflecting on her own poor boundaries with David, and how often she had probably been intrusive when she only meant to show him she loved him. It's as though she couldn't prove enough how much she cared, how much she would give. If only he would choose her… and he let her. He let her write his thesis, he let her support him financially and pay his half of the rent, he let her, took from her, used her. And it still wasn't enough because when the Bimbo walked into their lives, he left for someone who couldn't even spell "thesis." The Bimbo didn't have to "earn" him the way Janet had tried to do. She didn't have to be smart, handle his business, make him a priority, or abandon her own goals to make room for his… she had no goals or life to abandon. She had a tube top. That's all it took.

Janet has struggled with her primary drug of choice, food, as long as she can remember. Alone with her depressed mom and absent dad, food was reliable. It was a consistent avenue to comfort when she was lonely, happy, or frightened. She has made a lot of progress in recognizing the role of food in her life, and she's developed more coping skills and tools in recovery. However, when David left she felt as though all those tools had been pulled away from her, and she had returned to food as the ultimate source of nurturing. It's hard, because food as an addiction shows on the body – there is no hiding your self-soothing even if you don't eat in front of people. They can see you eat SOMETIME because you are clearly overweight. When you're overweight you're invisible in some ways.

Men certainly don't seem to see you, and women don't find you threatening. You take up more space, and body weight can ground you when the inside of you feels disconnected and weightless. The more Janet felt like she was broken into little pieces, the more she ate to become solid again.

Intellectually, Janet knows she has to be grounded inside, to trust herself and her judgment before she will let the weight go again. David's betrayal has shaken her to the core, and ripped open that isolated, invisible child festering inside her. His betrayal was proof she wasn't loveable, something she believed all her life because if she were, her parents would have paid attention to her.

Janet can feel herself beginning to get sucked under as her thoughts drift in this direction. She refocuses on the group to distract her. Focusing on the needs of others serves a purpose sometimes. It's a great survival tool.

When Janet gets back to her desk, she has a message from Amanda's Child Protective Services (CPS) worker asking for an update. She also has a message from Carolyn's husband about bringing the kids on Saturday. She decides to have Kym call Carolyn's husband, while she contacts the CPS worker about Amanda. She also has a couple of treatment updates to complete for the private insurance clients, which would then require her to call the insurance company and justify more treatment days in the facility. This was a hard part of her job and something she didn't have to do when she first come into treatment... back before Managed Care. Back then everyone was given 30 days of treatment, whether that they needed it or not. While this was not a great system, the insurance game now requires constant argument over medical necessity, and they are sometimes only approving 7 to 14 days. That is barely enough time to physically stabilize someone, and it certainly isn't rehabilitation. Then again, 30 days isn't either and treatment plans have to reflect this. Most of the ongoing work is done is in Outpatient and Aftercare facilities, leaving the truly residential treatment to its best use, stabilization and thorough assessment. It's a brain illness that doesn't reverse in a month.

Janet decides to stretch her legs and take a walk around the facility. As she rounds the corner she hears voices and looks out the window in time to see Paul (the client from Janet's fantasies) pull a leaf from intern Sarah's hair. Janet feels her heart start to race, her face turn red, and her stomach knot up. She flashes back to finding David with the skank after hearing them laughing behind a door. She has an overwhelming urge to race outside, slap Sarah across the face, and throw her to the ground. Janet feels so much rage she is shaking!

Fortunately Janet has some reality testing and knows she is over reacting and insane, so she heads into the bathroom to shut the door and sit on the floor until her breathing is normal. As she sits there, her chubby legs splayed out in front of her, she feels the tears start down her face. She feels helplessly overwhelmed by memories of David and the Bimbo, flashing images of them together and her feelings of humiliation. She feels like she wants to die – like she did when he first left.

She remembers being balled up on her therapist couch and saying, "I just can't do this anymore"

"What is THIS?" her therapist would ask.

"Everything, anything. I can't live without him – it's too hard. It's too dark by myself."

"You can do this. We will do this. I promise it will pass," her therapist would reassure her.

It has been two years since he left, and it shocks Janet that she is still so raw sometimes. Some days she barely thinks about it, and other days, like today, she gets triggered and feels like it was yesterday. It is exhausting.

Janet notices that her breathing is more even now, and she washes her face and heads back out to her office. When her adrenaline system jacks up like that she feels physically spent, as though she needs a nap. It strikes her that the clients are depending on the staff for sanity, reassurance and guidance. Yet with almost no provocation she was about to tackle Sarah and roll around with her on the grass. Thinking about this seems hilarious all of a sudden, and she knows she needs to tell someone, so she calls her sponsor, who also finds it hilarious. In fact, they imagine her fit over Paul erupting in mayhem – tearing the curtains off the wall, throwing the couches... by the end of the conversation Janet feels much better. Thank God she appreciates what a nut ball she really is!

The truth is most of the people who work in rehab are broken in some way. Ricardo with his cigarettes and fear of conflict, Eddie with his huge Big Gulps, Janet with her HoHo's, the Clinical Director with his rage and likely porn addiction. Recovery is a process for everyone, one layer at a time. The early wounds so many of them carry are core issues, deep issues that hang on long into recovery.

Janet's thoughts are interrupted by raised voices outside of her office. She pulls open her door in time to see Carolyn facing off with Raul of all people.

"You're a fat, stuck up bitch – you think you're better than everyone here!" Raul was yelling.

Carolyn looked pale, but was shaking in anger. "How dare you talk to me like that –people like you shouldn't be allowed to be in treatment with decent people like me!"

Ricardo rounds the corner with CD Tech Keisha. Ricardo exchanges looks with Janet, and engages Raul. "Raul, dude, you need to back it up." Raul turns to face Ricardo.

"I am tired of her disrespect!" Raul spit.

"I get that, man, I do. But the intensity is too much, you're upsetting the house. Let's go for a walk outside and calm down."

Raul shoots Carolyn a last hateful look, and follows Ricardo outside.

Janet turns to Carolyn, who is still shaking. "Come on in and calm down. Let me get you some water," Janet offers. Keisha checks in on the clients while Janet gets Carolyn situated. She asks Carolyn to talk about the situation.

"Honestly, I am not really sure how it started, "Carolyn begins. I know Raul was irritated with me earlier when I didn't pass the potatoes to him at lunch – it's like he thought I was hogging them. That's probably why he says I'm fat…" Tears fill her eyes. "I am fat. I know it." Carolyn whispers.

Janet can feel her stomach tighten up as she identifies with Carolyn's pain. "Then how did the yelling start?" Janet pursued.

I was sitting in the group room working on my autobiography assignment, and I guess I was sitting where he likes to sit for group. I just got here, so I didn't know that was his seat."

Clients, like students all over the world, establish "their" seats early on and it is understood that the seat belongs to them. It's silly, but it allows people to orient themselves in new situations and create a small comfort zone.

"He asked me to move, and I didn't feel like moving all my stuff, and then he started yelling at me."

"What was the part about 'decent people'?" Janet asked.

"I heard him bragging in the smoking area about stuff he does in prison, and it made me sick. I hate bullies and liars!"

Janet could see her way "in" now. "What is it about liars that makes you so angry?"

"I don't know. People who lie hurt people, make other people feel like fools."

"When you lied to your husband about drinking, was he hurt?"

Carolyn started to cry. "You think this is really about me? About my lying?"

"Could it be?" Janet probed.

"I guess I'm just as big a liar as Raul, then. I hate myself for it. I hate the look in my husband's eyes when he catches me. I feel so ashamed." Carolyn's head lowers at this point.

Janet and Carolyn continue their conversation for another

30 minutes, and Carolyn leaves shaken but with more self-compassion which hopefully she will extend to Raul. We'll see.

Ricardo joins Janet in a few minutes after he has Raul situated in time for the afternoon nutrition group to begin. This is a time for Ricardo and Janet to catch up on paperwork, including charting the recent altercation between Carolyn and Raul.

"Do you think we should write up an incident report?" Ricardo asks. Janet thinks a minute. "I am not sure it was an "incident" really. I am thinking it was two people in early recovery who got triggered. What do you think?"

"I agree. When I was talking to Raul it seemed really obvious that he's stressed out about the letter he mailed this morning to his baby's momma. He's really focused on it."

"Well, honestly, I am not too hopeful." Janet replies. "After all, he got the girl pregnant, and then disappeared because he was picked up on a violation. He's been gone a year – and no word to her. He hasn't contributed child support. It's possible she didn't even put his name on the birth certificate in order to get benefits."

Ricardo nods in agreement. "So what happened when you met with Marla yesterday? What's the deal?"

Janet thought about how much to say. "Kym was right about the trauma. She had a sexually and physically abusive step father, her bio father was out of the picture. She married her husband early to get out of the house, and there has been some domestic violence. She says she started drinking wine to make sex easier for her, and now she drinks to stay numb. I'm worried that there is no way she can get sober in her current marriage unless there is a drastic change."

"Do you think she is strong enough to make the change?" Ricardo asks.

"I don't think so. I think our best bet is to have Kym work with the husband to allow her to transfer to a Sober Living Home from residential to buy her more time to get stronger and develop more "self" before being thrown right back into the marriage."

"Has she ever made a police report about the violence?" Ricardo asked.

"No, she says it's 'only' pushing and shoving. She has slapped him a few times."

Ricardo shook his head. "That doesn't sound good."

Ricardo

Ricardo thought back to his own childhood, a childhood filled with alcohol-fueled yelling as his father would accuse his mother of infidelity. The mother of 5 children and sole caretaker of her own aging mother, his mother would have had no time for infidelity and it made her cry to be accused. "Whore!" his father would yell as he turned her purse over looking for evidence of another man. "Your mother is a slut!" he would yell at the children. "You probably aren't even my children!" he would holler as he staggered outside to the garage.

Ricardo learned to "check out" early on. First he discovered huffing, then pot, then he found heroin and he knew he had found the "solution" to managing the hatred he felt for his father, the grief he felt for his mother, and his shame at his own helplessness as he would watch his father shake and intimidate his mother. Ricardo understood Marla's dilemma because there was no way he could have lived at home and been sober. In fact all of his siblings are alcoholics and addicts except his sister, who married an alcoholic. He is the first one in the family to get clean, and he rarely goes home for family occasions even though his father is ill and mellower now.

"Maybe Kym can have a couple's session," Ricardo offers.

"It's so hard to know what is best. On the one hand she has to have enough solitude to develop as a person, on the other hand he has to buy in or he will sabotage everything we are trying to do. This is one of those times I'm happy that Kym is the family counselor and not me," Janet grins.

"Here, here," Ricardo laughs, and they both turn toward their computer screen to start charting.

Process Group

During the afternoon process group, Janet notices that Amanda seems somewhat brighter, and even smiles occasionally. Carolyn appears withdrawn and is slumped in her seat.

"Carolyn?" Janet checks in. "How are you doing?"

Carolyn barely glances at her.

"You look like you are carrying the weight of the world on your shoulders," Janet prompts.

"I keep thinking about what we were talking about earlier, and all the times I lied to my husband, Chris, and even bullied him to make him stop talking about my drinking. I feel so ashamed," she added, as tears begin to trickle down her cheeks.

"And that's not the way you were seeing yourself?" Janet asks.

"No! I really thought I was more in control. That I was hiding it better," says Carolyn tearfully.

Some of the clients smile.

"I totally get what you're saying," Paul says. "I really thought my fiancée couldn't tell when I was gacked! I thought I was just being creative and fun!" he laughs.

"I get it too", Marla says. "I was drinking mostly in the morning, so I figured if I had a nap, no one would know."

Carolyn nods with recognition.

"Then I started adding rum to my soda in the afternoon so I could have a couple more. When I would fight with my husband I always blamed him for being controlling - he was "making" me act like that! But, really I'm starting to think the alcohol was making it worse. I was more comfortable with him thinking I was a bitch than a drunk," she says.

Several of the clients laugh in identification.

"Yea, LIFE is the problem, DRUGS are the solution!" Janet laughs.

The process group continues, and the clients continue to explore ways they denied that addiction was an issue. In sobriety, they can see how futile it was, though it made sense at the time.

Janet

Janet wraps up her day by charting, and hits an AA meeting. As Janet leaves that night, she catches a glimpse of Ronnie standing near the exit and steels herself to greet him. Ronnie is a 6 foot 3 former ball player gone-to-seed who owns a local sketchy rehab. He sports a soft belly and thighs, full red-veined jowls, and one of those horrible little ponytails that balding men create when they gather up their remaining side hair and slick it back. The tail hangs limply, pointlessly. She decided to lead with a fist bump to avoid a hug that will make her want to shower later.

"Hey Janet," he opens with a sneer that implies, "I have a secret"

"Hey Ronnie", as she bumps his fist. "Whatcha doing here on a Wednesday night?"

"One of my counselors called in sick, so I decided to do some service and bring the guys to their outside meeting."

Janet immediately thinks of the rumor about his latest facility license suspension due to using the clients for a kitchen remodel and calling it "work therapy." She wonders if he is planning another room update.

"It's cool to see you still keeping your hand in the program, Dude. Take Care," she waves as she moves quickly to the door.

Ronnie represents the worst of rehab, the exploitive characters who prey on court-ordered clients and their parents or clients who feel powerless in the system. Operators like Ron stack them like cord-wood in Sober Living Home and rehab centers while offering minimal to no services. For instance, Ronnie's place charges $7,000 a month and instead of paying counselors, he's taking the clients to free AA/NA meetings 4 times a week. It's heart breaking and frustrating to the ethical counselors who work very hard for lower pay.

The system works however, because these same clients are poor self-advocates, have poor self-esteem and low expectations, and rarely want to work very hard on their own recovery. It's an implicit agreement, "You don't hold me accountable for my sobriety and give me my court letter, and I won't complain about your lack of services." If a client relapses, Ronnie is perfectly happy to take another $7,000, put them through the same 30 day program, and issue another completion certificate. He has two guys in his rehab center right now who have cycled 5 times each. Somehow their parents find the money, especially since he starts to give them a discount at the third round. What a guy!

Fortunately Janet spies Jonathon on the way out. Jonathon has one and a half years of recovery after graduating from her program. He grins at her and she lights up with pride and gratitude as she remembers how hard he worked for his 18 months. Jonathon entered recovery really unsure of his odds. Even at 23 years old his liver was 60% compromised by alcohol with an extensive family history of addiction. He had been referred after an alcohol poisoning that almost cost him his life. He came into treatment skeptical and clearly unable to imagine life without alcohol. Alcohol was the solution; life was the problem. As Janet worked with him week after week, including extending his stay in rehab, Jonathon sobered up enough to begin to feel the love of his family. He began to have hopes and dreams again – like Rip Van Winkle he woke up after 6 years and decided to begin his life. It has not been easy for him, and most of the guys he got sober with have relapsed. But Jonathon found a sponsor, a young guy, early on in the process and decided to use his support system. He decided to accept the love his family was offering him. When Janet thinks about Jonathan it's like getting second wind and she knows why she's spent her life in the trenches.

THURSDAY

When Janet arrives, the Clinical Director is roosting up in the office, which is never a good sign. Everyone feels more at ease when he is over in the administration building, because he brings a cloud of negativity with him.

"Good morning," she opens. "What's happening today?"

The Clinical Director turns to her and glowers. "One of the residents packed up and climbed out his window late last night, and the night guy, Carl didn't notice until this morning! We don't even know what time he left."

"Do you know which client left?" Janet asked.

"Ah, this guy Frankie."

"Frankie Flynn?" Janet was surprised. "I know Kym has been working really hard with the family, and I think he is due to graduate pretty soon. Do you know what set him off?"

"It's not like I'm in the loop," the Clinical Director spat. "I'm always the last one to know! I asked Carl to come in when he is done with med count."

Just then there's a knock and it's Carl. "I've been thinking about it, and when I did bed check I could swear he was there. He must have slipped out as soon as I left the room. I'm really sorry. I don't get why he climbed out the window. The front door is unlocked."

Janet often marveled at this phenomenon. Residential treatment centers are not locked from the outside, clients can leave whenever they decide to leave. They can pack up, call a cab, and meet the cab outside and take off. If they are court-ordered, it would be considered a probation or parole violation which would trigger a warrant. But the staff would never "prevent" a client from leaving if they were determined to go.

"What the hell happened last night, then? What set him off?" the Clinical Director demanded.

"When I got here for shift change, Eddie said that Frankie seemed upset after he got off the phone with his girlfriend. Eddie offered to talk about it, and Frankie blew him off. He just wanted to go outside and get a cigarette.

"What's with that relationship? Has she been coming to Family group?" the Clinical Director asked.

"I checked the log and she didn't come last week. It doesn't say why she didn't come. It was just his parents."

"I think Kym mentioned at Clinical Staffing that Frankie and his girlfriend have been fighting because she doesn't always call him back, or doesn't answer the phone when he calls. He is worried that she is hanging out with someone else. Kym met with the two of them and thought it had been resolved." Janet offered.

"Maybe not. I'll have Kym call the parents and let them know not to come to family group since he is no longer here. She'll have to do damage control because his mom is the hysterical type. I don't envy her," the Clinical Director observed.

"Boss, there is something else," Carl offered.

The Clinical Director hates it when the guys call him "Boss" – it's a prison term. "What is it?"

"I was doing med count this morning and a couple of the clients are missing 2 or 3 pills. I checked the pill log, and everything seemed to be okay, so I recounted and I still come up short."

"What kind of pills are missing?" the Clinical Director asks.

"Well, Stan is missing a couple of his pain meds he was issued for his dental work this week. Carla is missing a couple of her Lyrica for anxiety."

Janet and the Clinical Director exchange looks. "Why don't you bring the med's and the med log in here and Janet and I will do a recount and see if we can get to the bottom of this."

Carl looked relieved to hand the responsibility over to them. "You bet, boss. I'll be right back."

Treatment center staff prepare the medications for the clients to dispense to themselves since staff are not medical personnel. Sometimes they simply hand the client the pill bottle and the client takes the pills as prescribed, and sometimes they prepare the pills in cups and the clients take the cup from the staff.

Medications are logged every time they are admitted initially, and every time the client takes a pill. It is a running count, and the staff who is preparing the pills counts the remaining pills in the bottle every time.

When she gets off the phone, Janet sees the Clinical Director perched over the med book and beginning a pill count. The obvious answer is that someone on the staff is pilfering the pills and using them to get loaded. Having medication in treatment centers is necessary for the clients, but can seriously trigger the staff if they are not feeling strong in their own recovery program.

Janet thought through the staffing line-up. The other two people who do pill count are Eddie at night, and Jesse on the weekend. Carl does it in the morning. Neither Jesse nor Eddie have mentioned the pill discrepancy which may be because the pilfering is recent, and it was probably one pill at a time so the missing meds were chalked up to counting in a hurry. Carl had been off for a few days and was coming back with fresh eyes, so he caught it right away.

Chemical Dependency counselors do relapse. Being around the disease when it's active is stressful, and if counselors are doing poor self-care, they can resume old ways of thinking. It will show up in starting to be late, cheating on their time cards a few minutes at a time, taking too many personal calls, not enforcing the rules, sitting in the smoking area with the clients frequently and swapping war stories. Relapse can sneak up on you, and if one the counselors is taking the pills it means their mental shift started a while ago.

As Janet thinks about it, she reflects on Eddie in Clinical Staffing.

His demeanor was overly casual, and he was asking about Marla out of curiosity and not for clinical reasons. The more she thought about it she realizes that the clients looked forward to Eddie's shifts, and she begins to wonder if one of the reasons Frankie got into it with his girl is that he was abusing the phone time and Eddie wasn't setting limits. She could check the chore log and see if Eddie was checking off the chores or not, and chances are he has not stayed on top of it. The clients wouldn't complain about it, but they have been more irritable during the day when Janet and Ricardo enforce the house rules. Well, mostly Janet because Ricardo has a hard time with this also.

The Clinical Director finished the count, and Carl, was right. "So, who else does the pill count?" the Clinical Director asks as he checks the staffing schedule. "I see it's Eddie and Jesse. I guess we start with them," he says as he picks up the phone. He asks Jesse to meet with him in the afternoon, and Eddie to come in early for his evening shift for a conversation.

"How did they react to being asked to come in?" Janet asks.

"They were a little guarded, I think. Eddie a little more than Jesse, but that's also his nature," the Clinical Director observes. He frowns as he notes, "When I started working in the field clients weren't allowed any medication in treatment. There was none of this antidepressant bullshit. Everyone's depressed when they first get clean. It's just part of the deal. There weren't psych meds, and people seemed to get better anyway the longer they stayed clean. Letting all this shit in has led to this, you know," he says mostly to himself.

This was true when Janet first started in the field as well. Clients had to get off of their psychiatric meds in order to be admitted to a substance abuse rehabilitation center or a Sober Living Home. Standard wisdom was that you should wait at least two years into sobriety before prescribing psych meds to make sure you weren't medicating normal detox symptoms. However she remembers the relapse due to untreated depression and anxiety disorders, as well as ADHD and psychosis. Her memories of the non-med era weren't quite so fond, but thought better of saying so. No point, really.

"You have any thoughts about this? You're here the most," he asks.

"Actually, I do. I thought there was something a little off about Eddie at Clinical Staffing, and I suspect he hasn't been staying on top of the structure at night. It's a feeling I have – I would have to check the chore log to find out."

"Why don't you go ahead and do that. The more pieces I can put together ahead of time the better."

Janet left the room to check the chores. On her way down the hall she could hear Ricardo's Psychoeducation group, which meant that she could hear Ricardo talking and not the clients. He was right on with his information. He just wasn't very skilled at getting the clients to participate. He was too easily lured into personal disclosure by a client's question. He needs so badly to be heard, and Janet found herself wondering about Ricardo's childhood, and whether he was as invisible as she had been.

As Janet reviews the chore list she can see it's haphazard and inaccurate. Just a quick look in the bathrooms lets her know the clients aren't cleaning thoroughly, so her suspicions about Eddie are mounting. The problem is staffing, because if they let him go they'd only have one on-call person to pull in, which means Janet and Ricardo would have to pull extra shifts to cover the evenings until Eddie is replaced. Janet sighs at the thought, and feels a surge of anger at Eddie. No wonder she doesn't have a life!

Then again, it isn't Eddie's fault that she has so much free time. Truthfully, she could easily pull another shift and it wouldn't disrupt anything but her television schedule. She has been living a very limited lifestyle since David left. Work, meetings, therapy, her sponsor, and an occasional meal with a friend. Her world has become pretty small, almost to make her less of a "target" for more pain.

Janet enters the office and shares her findings with the Clinical Director, who raises his eyebrows while listening. She wishes he wasn't so fond of finding blame and "catching" the staff and clients. He seems to take some sort of satisfaction when he catches them in a discrepancy or in dishonesty. It's as though he is saying, "See, you didn't make a fool of me!"

This paranoia about being a fool is common with chemical dependency counselors. They tend to personalize clients behavior a great deal, seeing clients as trying to "pull one over" or "jerk me around" which may very well be true. But it's not personal. Addicts and alcoholics lie and deceive themselves and other people as an instinct. It is survival behavior, and it amazes her how often counselors forget this even though they were liars themselves! Actually, lying takes a long time to disappear in recovery. Some people continue lying and avoiding accountability for years after they stop drinking and using. Being emotionally honest is even harder for people to do consistently. It's too easy to say, "I don't mind," or "No problem" and then seethe inside or act out in some passive-aggressive manner later.

Janet is looking forward to the art therapy group this afternoon. When she has the time, she likes to sit in and participate in the art project of the day. Today they're making collages, her favorite, and she gets on top of her paperwork to make sure she is available when it is time.

She's interrupted by Kevin, who coughs gently to get her attention.

"Excuse me, Janet. Can I talk to you for a minute?" Kevin asks.

Janet turns to look at him standing there in his sweats and the same T-shirt he had on yesterday.

"Hi Kevin. Have you showered today? I think you had that shirt on yesterday." Janet opens.

"Uh, no. That's why I'm here. I can't find my shower shoes, and I'm afraid if I stand in the shower I will get fungus on my feet. I think fungus is really hard to get rid of, isn't it?"

"Well Kevin, I'm not sure, I never had fungus. What happened to your shoes?"

"I don't know. I thought I put them by my bed but now I can't find them," he says forlornly.

Janet hides her irritation as she gets up to follow him to his room to help him look for them. Kevin really does function like a 12 year old. She wonders if it is a cognitive delay, emotional trauma, a learning disability, or just laziness. She makes a note to check in with his parents about his developmental history.

After looking through the room, Janet figured out that the roommate has put them in the closet – where they belong, and Kevin seems relieved. He happily went off to shower and she returns back to the office to continue her paperwork and make some calls. One of the calls she had to make is to Frankie's probation officer because he is no longer on site, and the officer will have to put out a warrant. Janet always dreads these calls because not all the probation officers are sympathetic with treatment, and feel annoyed that they have to deal with addicts at all. Fortunately, this one is more open to treatment, so when she reports Frankie's absence he doesn't give her a hard time. He just thanks her and she returns to closing out Frankie's file with discharge notes.

Sarah pops in after Psychoeducation class, and Janet makes a decision to talk to her about what she saw between Sarah and Paul the day before. "Hey Sarah, let's go for a walk," Janet suggests.

As the women were in the backyard enjoying the sun, Janet opens the conversation.

"When I walked by the smoking area yesterday I saw you sitting closely to Paul and he was pulling a leaf out of your hair. It looked kind of intimate. What was going on there?"

Sarah turned pink. "Nothing. He just noticed that I had something in my hair and took it out. "

"How did you come to be alone with him in the smoking area?" Janet pursued.

"Well, he said he was feeling bummed and he would feel better if he could talk to me. That's what I'm here for, right?" Sarah asked defensively.

Janet could hear the edge in her voice. "Yes, we're here to help them. What do you notice about the way he acts with you?"

"What do you mean?" Sarah seems puzzled.

"You know, what he talks about, how physical he is with you, how he makes you feel when you are with him."

Sarah thought a moment. "Well, he seems like he's a really good listener, like he's interested in learning about me. He said he was thinking about being a counselor himself and that maybe I could give him some pointers."

"Uh huh," Janet nods.

"And he does have a great smile. Are you trying to find out if I have a crush on him?"

"I suspect you probably do. But I am not surprised because he seems to `work' most of the women around him," Janet said.

"That's true," Sarah realized. "I even heard Marla laughing this morning with him, and she never laughs!"

"Exactly," Janet said. Do you have the sense that he is trying to get you to like him?"

"Well, now that you mention it, yes he is. But he makes himself easy to like!" Sarah smiled.

"That's a special skill set he has no doubt learned to survive. What's important is for you not to take it personally. He runs that energy with every woman in the house, including me."

"You too?" Sarah's eyes widened.

"Me too. In fact, I was considering rolling you around on the grass when I saw you yesterday because I had a flash of jealousy."

"Oh my God!" Sarah was laughing, "Really?"

"Not really," Janet lied. "But I did notice the two of you and had a reaction. I think it's because part of his shtick is to make you feel like you're the only important person in the room."

"That's true," Sarah agreed. "Okay. Thanks for bringing it to my attention so I can watch for it. I'm sure you're right that it's a pattern. Do you think he's a sex addict?"

"I'm not sure," Janet said. "I wouldn't be surprised. If his drug of choice is meth, and I think it is, there are a lot of meth people who act out sexually with porn and other alternative sexual stuff they wouldn't try sober. It's worth checking into because it is a common cross-addiction. I'll mention it to Ricardo."

Art Therapy

On the way in to the office, Janet spies the art therapist setting up for group, and she feels her heart lift. She seats herself among the clients at the edge of the table, grabs a blank piece of paper, and waits for instructions. The art therapist, Anne, explains, "The purpose of today's collage activity is to find images that represent you're here-and-now experience, what it feels like to be you, and then find images that represent who you want to be – how you see yourself in recovery. Use your instinct, don't overthink it. Use images even if you aren't sure why you are including them, but you feel drawn to them."

Anne turns on some warm background music, and after the initial giggling and rustling, the clients start thumbing through the magazines concentrating on the images and even phrases that jump out at them.

Janet quickly loses herself in the task, grabbing National Geographic and Travel magazines. She realizes that she keeps being drawn to stories about unearthed mummies, sand-covered ruins, and even shipwrecks. As she tears the pages out she begins to see obvious themes, and soon her page is filled with earthy skeletons and ruins. Her page is grey with sepia tones, and the page is almost covered without images of who she would be in recovery. She has to go back through the magazines to look for images with color; images of life. The best she can come up with are safari scenes, still sandy but with vegetation and animals. She also manages to glue a small ocean photo onto the side of the page because water is always so comforting to her.

Janet realizes that she will not be able to share her collage with the group - she is the counselor dammit! She knew the art therapist would immediately spot her depression and the paucity of life on her page. Janet suddenly feels too exposed, and excuses herself to make a phone call.

Back in her office she lays the picture out on her desk and studies it. It's accurate, and she feels her heart start to ache as she recognizes her inner world in the images. Hearing footsteps she folds up her paper and shoves it in her desk.

Jesse

It was Jesse arriving for his meeting with the Clinical Director. Jesse is a 32 year old CD Tech currently in college for the first time studying to be an alcohol and drug counselor. Jesse went through treatment for prescription drug addiction 3 years ago, and found the counselors compassionate and inspiring. He wants to give back to the field that he credits with his recovery. He is active in Narcotics Anonymous, plays on a sober softball team, and sponsors 3 newcomers. He recently left the Sober Living Home to room with 2 guys he met in the program. His family is worried about him because he's so immersed in recovery he doesn't seem to have a balanced life. Even his sponsor is concerned that he might "burn out" now that he is working in addiction treatment. At the same time, Jesse is the happiest he's ever been and the call from the Clinical Director has him worried.

Janet could see the anxiety on his face. "Hey, Jesse. Are you here for your meeting?"

"Yes," he replies. "What's this about? Have I screwed something up? I've been thinking all day about my last shift and I can't think of anything major I may have forgotten. Is there a complaint about me?"

"It's going to be okay," Janet reassures him. "The Clinical Director wants to talk to you guys about medication count protocol. You'll be fine."

Jesse looks relieved. "Oh, okay, I had some questions anyway. Thanks a lot, Janet," he calls as he heads to the Clinical Director's office.

Janet gets on the computer to complete her treatment plans, but keeps getting interrupted by pop up advertising give-a-ways, or pop ups asking her to complete surveys. It's incredibly aggravating! She shuts down and reboots the computer to make it disappear, but shortly it returns. Groaning inside, she knows the computer probably has a virus, so she puts a call into the Clinical Director.

"Hi, sorry to interrupt you. I think we have a problem on the computer. I'm having a hard time accessing my treatment forms, and I keep getting weird pop ups. Did you notice this on the computer when you were here yesterday?" Janet asks.

"No, I didn't use the computer yesterday, so I can't say. Did you try to restart it?" he asks.

"Yes, and they keep coming back. Can you call the IT guy to come over and take a look at it? I'm afraid it's going to get worse, and I don't want to lose all our data like last time." Janet explains.

"Have you people been backing the damn thing up? We had an agreement last time this happened?" he demands.

"Honestly, it's probably been hit and miss. However, I've stored the important stuff in the cloud, so worst case scenario we can retrieve our master documents."

"I paid for a new protection system when we had the thing repaired last time. Have you guys been going to weird places? Has Ricardo been on Facebook again?"

Janet laughed. "He may have but that's not where it came from. Let's get the guy out here and see if he can figure it out. I'll do the best I can in the meantime. Thanks for your help." Janet says as she is hanging up.

Jesse pokes his head in the door. "Wow, Dude really has a stick up his ass today, huh?" he smiles. "I think he was trying to get me to confess that I'm palming the meds and taking them myself! Not my thing anymore."

"Yes, he's on a tear. But missing meds are a big deal. So, he's puffing around, but his point's a good one," Janet offered. "*Why do I defend that jackass?*" she asks herself.

"Well, he'll figure it out. He's good at that. I'm headed to soft ball practice, so I'll see you later!" he calls out as he leaves the building.

Janet feels encouraged after her encounter with Jesse, because her instincts were right. Jesse was way too committed to his program to jeopardize his recovery or his job. It probably wasn't going to go so well with the evening counselor, Eddie.

Eddie

Eddie is a 42 year old recovering methamphetamine addict, clean for 12 years. He stopped going to meetings when he started working in the field full time. He states, "I work all day in recovery. I need a break from it after work." This is a common belief amongst recovering counselors, and it misses the point. Eddie is assisting other people to work THEIR program, he is not working his own recovery. This is a confusion between being a sponsor and being in recovery. A sponsor works with recovering people as part of Twelve Step. Alcohol and Drug Counseling is a job, and with it come the stressors of a job. In addition, you are providing services to people who often "don't want what you have" and may even fight you when you try to assist them. People who work in recovery need MORE program to stay level, not less. Eddie's lack of self-care is showing up at home.

Eddie's wife has recently asked him for a divorce. She's tired of his moodiness and lack of emotional availability. She says she's lonely in the marriage, and feels like they are roommates. She wants more in the relationship and now that the kids are in high school she feels she can go back to work to contribute financially. Eddie has distanced himself from his recovery support system, and he is too embarrassed to talk to his brother. He feels ashamed, angry, and confused and is having trouble managing his feelings of depression. Eddie's in trouble, and he has forgotten his recovery solutions so using seems more and more like an option.

When Eddie arrives for the meeting with the Clinical Director before his shift, he has a bad feeling. He knows he's been "screwing up" and has been hoping to pull himself together before anyone finds out. As soon as he sees the expression on the Clinical Director's face he knows.

"Hi Eddie, thanks for coming in early. I have been calling you guys in because there seems to be a problem with the med count, and I'm hoping you can help me out," the Clinical Director begins.

Eddie sits in silence.

"Eddie, are you okay? I need your help with this. Is there anything you want to tell me?"

"Am I fired?" Eddie asks quietly. His head is hanging and his shoulders are rolled forward. How is he going to tell his wife, who is already talking about divorce, that he got fired?"

"Eddie, are you using again, man? Talk to me about it. Let's figure something out." The Clinical Director is surprisingly calm.

"I haven't started shooting meth yet. Just some pills here and there. Nothing steady. Just when I need to stop thinking and I need to sleep," Eddie shares.

"What are you thinking about that seems so heavy to you?" the Clinical Director asks.

"My old lady's tellin' me she's sick of my ass. Talks about leaving and taking the kids with her. She says I'm like a dark cloud in the house all the time, and she can't take it anymore." Eddie said, defeated. It sounds even worse when he says it out loud.

The Clinical Director was quiet, and remembering when his wife said the same thing to him last year. So he asked, "Eddie, do you think you might be depressed? Sometimes when men get depressed we get pissed off instead of sad. I've been there."

"You have?" Eddie was surprised. "You've been clean a long time. How come you still get depressed?"

"Oh, I have my reasons," the Clinical Director smiles. "Right now, we need to address yours. What I want to do is put you on a medical leave so you can collect disability while you are out. We can have you see our doctor and get the paperwork. I want you to see him about your depression and you need to stabilize your relapse. I'm really glad you aren't using meth, but you came damn close. When your doctor releases you and says you are ready to come back to work I need to reassign you so you are no longer doing the med count. How does that sound?"

Eddie had tears of relief in his eyes. "I'm not fired? Thank God."

"You need to get your ass to a meeting tonight, and get a sponsor. It worked 12 years ago and it will work again. Especially if you also see the doctor." The Clinical Director adds.

"What about my group tonight?" Eddie worried.

"It's handled, don't worry. Your main job right now is to take care of yourself. We'll still be here."

Eddie gathers his coat and walks to the door. "Thank you," he says with tears of relief.

Janet watches Eddie leave, and she's relieved that he seems okay. However, it also meant that someone would have to cover his group, so she figured she'd better grab the evening curriculum and see what she would be covering. No matter what, she was going to have to process Eddie's absence with the group. She decides to check in with the Clinical Director to figure out how to phrase it, though she suspects it would be a "medical leave" if he wasn't fired. From the lack of raised voices, she's betting on a medical leave.

She heads to group with a smile on her face, realizing why she "defends the jackass" after all.

Evening Psychoeducation

The clients look surprised to see Janet, expecting Eddie for his usual shift. When you're in residential treatment you surrender a great deal of control. You're scheduled seven days a week, and clients are quick to memorize counselor shifts to feel some sense of orientation and predictability. They also memorize counselor temperaments, much like children are aware of parent temperaments, and choose their behavior strategies accordingly. Eddie has established himself with loose boundaries, and some of the clients exploit his lack of attention to detail.

"Where's Eddie?" Angel asks. "I saw him here earlier."

"Eddie is going to take some personal time for himself, so Ricardo and I will be handling evening group for now."

"Is he okay?" Josie asks with concern.

"I promise he is going to be just fine. You know, counselors have lives too, and sometimes we need to take care of ourselves the way we encourage you to do."

"We are too much for him!" Paul laughs.

"That's interesting, Paul. What would be too much about YOU for Eddie?" Janet asks.

Paul frowns, "I was just teasing."

Janet smiles at him. "So we're going to talk about Triggers tonight." She turns to the white board and draws four columns.

Activating Event   Thought   Behavior   Consequence

"Activating events are things that raise our emotions. It can be something that happens outside of us, or a thought or feeling inside of us.

When the event happens we have a thought about it which then triggers a feeling about it. Then we DO something which is the consequence.

Let's explore this with something that happened recently. Any of you triggered to use lately?"

Everyone smiles.

Amanda raises her hand. "I wanted to use when I heard I wasn't going to get my son back."

"Amanda, do you mind if we use that situation? It's pretty personal." Janet asks.

"I don't mind. Maybe it will help me."

Janet smiles encouragingly at her. "Okay," and she turns back to the Board.

Activating Event

"Amanda learns she will not get her son back right away. Amanda, what was your thought about that?"

"I don't remember, I just felt horrible... I know. I thought, `I will never get Joey back.'"

"What did you tell yourself about WHY you wouldn't get Joey back?"

"Because I don't deserve to because I'm an addict," her eyes tear up.

Thought

"I don't deserve Joey, he's never coming back."

"Do you remember the feeling you had when you had that thought? I know this is hard, and you're doing great."

Amanda sniffed, "I felt like, 'Why bother'?"

"Do you mean getting clean or living?" Janet asked. She could see the room tensing as she asked this question.

"I don't know. Maybe both." Amanda admits.

"I can absolutely understand that. Can anyone else relate to this feeling?" Janet asks the group.

There was a lot of nodding.

Behavior

"Okay. What did you DO then, when you felt that way?"

"Well I was here, so I didn't use."

"No, you didn't. You did something else, remember?" Janet prompts.

"I talked about it in women's group!" Amanda smiles tearfully.

"That's right."

Consequence

Talked about it in group, stayed clean.

"What did you think after you talked about it with us?"

"I thought maybe it could change."

"So what did you feel?"

"I felt a little more hope."

"And what did you do next?"

I made a card for Joey," Amanda smiles.

Janet looks around the group. "Do you see how this works? Now I want you to get out your handout and sketch a situation out for yourself. After a few minutes we'll talk about what you came up with."

She watches them concentrate, and migrates over to Raul to help him with his writing in case he gets stuck. So much of traditional treatment is reading and writing oriented, which can be a real disadvantage for people like Raul. Some clients have so much shame they act out in treatment and get discharged rather than admit their reading and writing limits. Fortunately, Raul has developed enough self-esteem in prison politics that he could handle asking for help.

After group, it was going to be chore time, so Janet found the chore list to make sure the clients were completing the chores they were assigned. She could feel the annoyed vibe from the slacker clients, which amused her a little.

The rest of the evening was quiet, and Carl relieved her at 10:30, which made it a 14 hour day, and 8:30 am arrival tomorrow.

"Janet, girl, you had a long one. Eddie's out for a while? Man I hope he finds his way back." Carl says.

"I have a lot of hope he will. It's been a full day for sure."

"How are they doing?"

"They weren't too thrilled about chore time. I think I heard Kevin call me a `chore Nazi'," she smiles.

Carl chuckles. "Yea, that was getting a little lax, but I stay in my hula hoop, as my Alanon wife says."

"It might have been helpful to have known, Carl. Really! We might have been able to help Eddie sooner."

Carl looks defensive. "I'm not a snitch, man."

"Carl, it's not snitching. It's an intervention. Besides you did a great job with the med situation," Janet adds.

Carl looks mollified. "I'll think about the intervention thing, Janet. I guess I still have to let go of some of my old mentality."

"Don't we all?" Janet smiles. "Take care, I'm taking off."

Carl

Carl is 32 years old and has been clean a year and a half after spending much of his young adulthood in and out of prison for sales charges. He got clean through the Salvation Army, completing their 1 year work program. Carl struggles with the Twelve Step meetings, often because he is the only person of color in the meeting. He was reintroduced to his childhood faith in Chapel while at the Salvation Army and has continued to stay clean through Celebrate Recovery at his church.

Carl is struggling with not using any substances at all, and has thought about using pot. Working in treatment also keeps him sober, because he sees the real consequences of using daily and doesn't ever want to lose his freedom again.

Carl makes his rounds every hour or so, checking to make sure the clients are in their rooms. When clients can't sleep, which is normal in early recovery, they will often wander out and chat with Carl for a while. This is his favorite part of the job, and it also helps keep him awake. When everyone sleeps it is a long night, and staying awake is a challenge. Fortunately he can surf the web at Janet's desk.

It is about 12:30 a.m. and Carl hears, "Carl?" as Kevin shuffles out of his room.

"Hi buddy. Having a hard time sleeping?"

Kevin nods. "My mind keeps racing, and I can't shut it off. Do you think a cigarette would help?" he asks.

Carl thinks a minute. "I don't think so. I think that's why they cut off your smoking at 10:30." Carl answers.

"Well, I saw you smoking, and it's after 10:30," Kevin challenges.

Carl laughed. "Well that's true. But I am trying to stay awake, right?"

Kevin looked annoyed. "Why did you laugh when I challenged you? Sometimes I think no one takes me seriously."

"Why do you think that is, Kevin?"

"I don't know. Because I'm younger than other people? Because I am a pill addict and not a heroin addict?"

"Maybe. I wonder if it might have to do with the fact that you tend to complain a lot."

Kevin appears to think about this. "I don't think I complain any more than anyone else."

"Well, you complain to the staff. Everyone else complains to each other ABOUT the staff. So it can look like you are tattling – like you're a snitch."

"That's not fair! I am not complaining about other people. I am complaining about myself." Kevin says defensively.

"You know, I'm not a counselor or anything. But I wonder, did you get a lot of attention when you were sick as a kid?" Carl asks.

Kevin nods. "I suppose. My mom worried a lot about my health. Especially after my Grandma died."

"So she started hovering maybe, afraid of losing you next?"

"That's true, I'm sure. Do you think that's important? Why I complain?"

"Only you really know, Kevin. But I'd give it some thought. Maybe talk to Janet about it during your one-on-one."

Kevin was starting to look sleepy. "Thanks, Carl. I think I'll try to sleep again."

"Okay, bro'. Sleep well."

FRIDAY

Assignment Group

Janet starts the day with Assignment Group. During the course of treatment, clients are asked to complete assignments such as autobiographies that connect their using to their life choices; powerlessness and unmanageability questionnaires; or a relapse prevention plan. In assignment group clients read their assignments and remain open to feedback. The stories are often familiar ones, and clients begin to develop compassion for themselves as they extend compassion to others who have suffered in similar ways. Clients can choose to keep some of the more deeply personal sections of their stories (i.e. rape or molestation) private from the group. The point is to connect the dots between life consequences and using alcohol and drugs.

It's Paul's turn to share his autobiography, and Janet takes note of her particular curiosity in this case. She knows meth is his drug of choice, and has a vague idea about his using history. But he's on Ricardo's case load so she hasn't been privy to his details.

Paul opens his autobiography with a charming smile, imme-diately engaging the group. "*It really is a gift.*" Janet thinks to herself. As he begins the outline of his early life and the con-stant relocations due to his father's gambling, his use of charm to adapt to new situations makes more sense. He was constantly starting over, so had very little solid attachment except for his mother who worked long hours due to his father's fluctuating income. Sometimes they lived in gated communities, and some-times in two bedroom apartments in sketchy parts of town. Paul discovered alcohol and drugs to help him manage the constant unsettled status of his life. Alcohol helped him feel calm and relaxed, and meth helped him stay up and motivated; until it became an addiction and took over his life. Married and divorced twice, he is currently engaged. Like his father he is charming and emotionally unavailable. He always has secrets. Paul has no idea what intimacy is and is unsure what his fiancée means when she says she has a hard time getting close to him. "I'm an open book," he says with a grin.

It is clear to Janet that Paul is unaware of how much he has relied on charm rather than developing a strong internal sense of self. No wonder he feels so unmoored — like there is no solid ground. This is a common experience for addicts. In fact, some theorists suggest that the addiction is really an attempt to create a secure attachment we can trust.

Janet listens carefully to the feedback the clients offer Paul, noting that they see his void inside but aren't sure how to describe it. But they do recognize it, that's for sure.

Gently, Janet wonders aloud, "Paul, when you are alone with yourself, and it's just you, how solid do you feel?"

"I'm not sure what you mean. You mean, do I feel safe?"

"That's close," Janet says. "Do you feel more like you are anchored to the ground or more like a balloon and you could fly away?"

"Definitely the balloon," he laughs. "Why, is that bad?"

"No, it's not bad. But is makes me wonder if you use alcohol to feel more anchored or meth to feel more direction instead of floating aimlessly, like a balloon."

Paul gives this some thought. It was obvious other group members were also thinking about this.

"I think you might be right," he offers. "It's so normal for me to feel this way I never thought about it before. Do you think the balloon thing might be why my fiancée says it is hard to get close to me, and that I am only real when I drink?"

"Exactly!" Janet clapped her hands. "We are going to need to work on mindfulness techniques — tools you can use to stay in your own body without having to use alcohol or meth."

Paul looks relieved.

Janet hears a few more assignments, admiring the honesty and emotional risks clients take in treatment. *"God, I love what I do,"* she finds herself thinking.

After group Janet returns to the office and the computer guy was finishing up. "So, did you work your magic?" she asked.

The computer guy, Jim, grinned at her. "Indeed I did. I cleaned your system, and I found your problem."

"And?"

"We'll someone here has been spending a lot of time on porn sites. They are notorious for leaving Trojan viruses when they are opened. Want to see the history?" he offered.

Janet was just staring at him. "Okay, I guess," as she peered over his shoulder. "Oooh, that's some nasty stuff! Can you figure out what time and day the websites were being accessed?"

"Absolutely. Here… looks like you have a night owl! 1 a.m., 3 a.m., 4 a.m. I can give you a list of the days and times if you want."

It was obvious to Janet it was either a client accessing the computer, which means they had to have their passwords, or obviously the graveyard guy, Carl. Actually, it grossed her out thinking about Carl rubbing one out sitting in her chair. She grimaced.

"What is it?" Jim asked.

"It's probably our night guy, and I'm getting grossed out picturing him doing himself sitting here. What if he got some on the chair?" she says as she glances down into the seat.

Jim laughs. "Okay, that's pretty gross. Do you want me to call the Clinical Director?"

"No, I'll do it," Janet says. "We have to talk about what to do now. Just send the bill directly to the main office. Thanks for fixing it."

Ricardo walks in after leading Community group with Jorge and sees the look on Janet's face.

"You look like you smell something bad! What's going on? Did the computer guy leave?"

"Yeah. Apparently we have viruses due to porn sites. When we looked at the days and times it looks like it's Carl. I am so grossed out right now."

"Why?" Ricardo laughs, "Cause homeboy was getting some sitting in your chair?"

"Very funny," Janet mutters.

Ricardo just shook his head. "So, have you called the Clinical Director yet?" he asks.

"No, Jim just left. I guess I have to. Boy, this is going to be awkward."

"I have your back. I'll sit here for support," says Ricardo.

"Wanna sit in my chair?" Janet asks with a grin.

"Lord no, homegirl. Savin' it all for you," he sings.

Janet places the call to the Clinical Director. "Hi there. The computer guy just left and he was able to clean the machine and get things working the way they should."

"That's great. Was he able to figure out the problem?"

"Well, yes. Apparently someone has been watching porn on the computer and downloaded some viruses."

"God dammit!" came his predictable response. "Who the hell is it? Could he tell?"

"It looks like it was probably Carl because it was in the early hours and on his days. What do you want to do?"

"I want to call his horny ass down here for a chat. I want you to change the password to the computer and only tell Ricardo and Jesse. Got it?!" he shouted.

"Okay. He's supposed to be on shift tonight. Ricardo is already covering Eddie's shift, so what should we do?"

"Carl is going to do his own damn shift, and he's not going to have access to the computer. I wonder if he's been doing his rounds like he claims. Maybe that kid, Frankie, took off when Carl was jacking off!"

"Good point," Janet acknowledges, feeling sorry for Carl. There is nothing worse than a self-righteous hypocrite. It was obvious from the way the Clinical Director looks down Kym's shirt and watches Sarah's ass that he's no stranger to porn himself! "So, you'll call him?" she asks.

"I'm on it now. Thanks." he says and abruptly hangs up.

Ricardo was on the phone with Angel's parole officer. Apparently, Angel was not up front about his upcoming court date, and didn't mention the restraining order awarded to his son's mother. Ricardo sounds aggravated by Angel's lack of disclosure, and when he hangs he up blurts out,

"God, why are they such liars?! I thought we had a bond going, man. How come he lied to me? He even asked ME to call his ex and suggest couple's counseling on family day without mentioning the restraining order!"

"Ricardo, it's not personal. These guys have been lying forever; they never fully disclose at the beginning. You know that."

"Yeah, I know." Ricardo agrees. "But I thought Angel and I were on the same wave length. He reminds me so much of me when I first got clean."

"Maybe that's the problem, "Janet suggests. "Maybe you were seeing too much of yourself in the guy. I know I've done that. It can happen."

Ricardo considers this for a minute. "You're probably right. Last time Carolyn was here she hassled me so much that when Angel showed up, and seemed so willing, I may not have asked enough questions. I know from my own history that convicts never offer information. I would have to have asked him a direct question to get him tell me, if he was going to tell me at all."

"So maybe he didn't lie. Maybe he just didn't trust you enough to offer it up?" Janet asks.

"Yeah. Sometimes I forget they don't trust us. To them we're just one more person in the system."

"It's harder for them. It's riskier for them to believe that we are going to be different from all the others," Janet observes.

Ricardo nods. "Yeah, just because I know my heart's in the right place doesn't mean they know that. Thanks Janet. I felt like going off on that guy."

"That's why we do this as a team, bro," Janet says as she offers him a fist bump. "So, Ricardo, it's your turn to pick up Eddie's shift tonight. I took it last night."

"I figured that. I told my wife this morning. I hope the Clinical Director is calling someone – we're going to need a break next week."

"Dude, we need a break NOW!" Janet laughs. "TGIF!"

THUD! They jump up and run out to the client lounge and find Karen splayed out on the floor. Janet races over and checks her pulse, she is breathing and passed out. "Karen," Janet calls, "Karen!"

Karen opens her eyes and looks up.

"Honey, you are pale as a sheet. What happened?"

"I don't know. I got up to go to my room and the next thing I remember is your voice calling me."

"Lay still and Ricardo will call the paramedics." Ricardo already has his cell phone out and is dialing. Janet hears him give the address as she sits with Karen and calms the other clients. Within 5 minutes the paramedic are there, strapping Karen to a gurney to take her for testing.

Karen had been admitted on Sunday after her parents had dropped her off. She's a thin, guarded meth addict who even at 24 looks like her life has been very hard. Facing charges for possession and assaulting an officer, she agreed to treatment at her attorney's suggestion. Janet had completed the initial intake and knew Karen's only current medication was for high blood pressure.

Janet calls Karen's mom, who's listed as the emergency contact, and lets her know where Karen has been transported. Janet will pop over at lunch time to check on her, or take her back to the center if she's ready for discharge.

Janet grabs an incident report form to document the fainting incident and paramedic involvement and places it in Karen's file.

Ricardo seems to be lost in thought at his desk. He turns to Janet and asks, "I am supposed to talk about Communication styles in Psychoeducation group. I am thinking I would like to use this incident and pick a better topic. What do you think about `The physical consequences of addiction' lecture? "

Janet nods in agreement. "You might as well talk about it while the paramedics are on their mind. Their families have witnessed this type of thing so many times. It will be interesting to see how they feel being on the other end; how they would guess their family felt when they were called to the hospital or called the paramedics themselves. It could get pretty real in there. I envy you."

Ricardo grinned. "Bring it, baby," he says over his shoulder as he heads to the group room.

Janet places a call to the Clinical Director to fill him in, and winds up leaving a message. She decides to enter her treatment plans and call Kevin's doctor about his medication. Janet has been worried that Kevin's doctor may not know that he is seeing both an internal medicine guy and a psychiatrist. Prescription medication addicts like Kevin are incredibly sophisticated in their ability to manage multiple doctors and pharmacies. Kevin may not be able to find his shower shoes, but he can always find some Vicodin! It's entirely possible that he has other prescriptions stashed to use "later" and doctors are completely unaware of each other. It's also possible to find an independent pharmacy that is not hooked into the computer system the way Rite Aid and Walgreen's are. Janet, armed with signed releases, begins placing calls in the inevitable game of phone tag.

Karen

Upon finishing her last treatment plan, Janet looks up at the clock and realizes it's time to head over to the hospital to check on Karen. Ricardo has returned from group, so she signs out and makes the trip across town. Karen will be admitted overnight for tests, so Janet is directed to her room. Karen is resting and watching TV when Janet enters.

"So, Karen, what have they found so far?"

"Well, it may have to do with my medication."

"You're taking high blood pressure medication, right? Didn't you take it this morning?"

"Yes, I did. But they think the dosage may be too high, so my blood pressure is too low."

"Karen, did you tell your doctor you were using methamphetamine?" Janet asks.

Karen grins sheepishly, "No. So when the medicine didn't work he kept upping the dosage."

"Well no wonder you passed out! Why didn't you say something to him?"

"Well, what was I supposed to say? 'Hey doc, did I mention I'm a tweaker?' I was afraid he wouldn't treat me anymore and I needed the medicine."

Janet laughed, "I see your point. So they're going to keep you to see if the meth has done any additional damage to your heart?"

"Yeah, that's right. Will you come and get me tomorrow?"

74

"I'll come as soon as they call me. Is your mom coming?"

"She called my room and said she would head over after work."

"Okay. Get some rest. I'll check on you later and pick you up tomorrow."

"Thanks Janet… really," Karen smiles.

Process Group

Janet returns to the office in time to conduct her afternoon process group. The clients shuffle in, taking their usual seats. Out of the corner of her eye Janet spies Marla and Paul moving their chairs a little closer. She decides to keep her eye on them and see what develops. Janet opens with a check in, and sits quietly waiting to see what develops. Not surprisingly Amanda asks about Karen.

"Is she okay? She looked really pale."

"She's okay and going to stay overnight for more testing," Janet assures her. "What were you feeling when you saw her fall?"

"I was scared. I remember times when I would fall, but I wouldn't faint. I was just clumsy."

"Did you ever hurt yourself?" Janet asks.

"Not very badly. Mostly I would be embarrassed and feel really stupid."

"Anybody else have feelings come up when Karen fainted?"

"I was reminded of a friend of mine who OD'd in front of me once. It scared the shit out of me," Angel says.

"What did you do?"

"Well, we were loaded and shit, so we left and called 911 to tell them where he was."

"Were you sure he was dead?" Janet asks.

"Yeah he was dead! I wouldn't leave a homey alive like that," he says irritably. Janet wonders about this to herself.

"How did a scare like that effect your using?" she probes.

"Honestly, I probably used more the next couple of days. It really freaked me out," he admits.

Kevin is looking horrified. "I never think about dying from my medication - it's prescribed! My doctor would never give me something that would kill me!" he says heatedly.

Everyone looks a little surprised at his naiveté, including Janet.

"Kevin, you're here because you abuse your medication. You don't take it as prescribed. You're right, the medicine won't kill you as prescribed, but you take way more than the doctor recommends. You absolutely COULD die from opiates if you take too many. Especially since you take benzodiazepines like Xanax and Valium with them. How do you feel as I am telling you this?" Janet asks.

Kevin looks pale. "I don't know. I guess I don't want to believe you."

Josie interrupts, "Kevin, do you remember how Ricardo said in Psychoed that drugs like alcohol and opiates slow our breathing? If we use too much we will stop breathing?"

Kevin just stares at her. Then he slowly nods. "Oh, shit. You're telling me that I could have killed myself?"

"How does that make you feel, Kevin?" Janet insists.

"It makes me want to cry." He says with tears in his eyes. "I love taking those pills. I still want to take those pills. But I don't want to die."

"Anyone else relate to that?" Janet threw out to the group.

Mike speaks up, "Man, I have the same problem. I love to drink. I love to check out and stop feeling. At the same time, I don't want to die anymore. But when I drink, I can't stop drinking, so even though I may not consciously be wanting to die, I might accidently kill myself anyway. It's not worth the risk to me anymore."

"Anymore." Carolyn says. "You said you didn't want to die anymore."

"That's right."

"How did that happen? How did you stop wanting to die?" Carolyn's voice was pleading.

"I stopped wanting to die because I hadn't died yet despite my best efforts. So I figured that maybe there was some reason I was supposed to still be here. Once I started thinking that, I started being a little curious about what that reason might be."

"Like wanting to know how the story ends?" Janet asks.

"Just like that," Mike smiled. "But Carolyn, I want you to know I get it. I get what hopelessness feels like. I get that it probably seems too hard right now. These people here can help you if you let them. You still have kids to raise, so you have even more purpose than I did."

Carolyn nodded. "I know that intellectually. I know you are right. And sometimes I still wish I could just not wake up. But I wouldn't hurt myself on purpose because of the kids."

Other members of the group shared similar moments of despair, and Carolyn was able to see how universal her wish to "not wake up" is in addiction. She is truly not alone.

As Janet winds up the group she notices Paul drawing on Marla's notebook, and she looks preoccupied with him. This sets off multiple alarm bells for several reasons, each of which shoots through Janet's head in rapid-fire succession:

1. Marla is probably angry at her controlling husband, and a flirtation with another man might seem like a good way to teach him a lesson.

2. Her husband is volatile and controlling, and could cause a problem for the weekend staff.

3. Paul is engaged to someone who might spot the flirtation immediately since she is already having trouble feeling close to him.

4. Paul is running the same game he has run a thousand times, and Marla may not know it's a game.

5. Over-association distracts them from their personal recovery efforts, and is often a way to get a high. Particularly since they know it is not acceptable in the treatment setting.

6. If the flirtation grows, the house will have to keep a "secret" which will make them act out with each other due to their discomfort and anxiety.

Janet decides to meet with Marla and talk with her about it since Marla is on her caseload. She waves Marla into her office after group and closes the door.

"Hi Marla, how are things going for you this week? I know we talked about some tough parts of your history a few days ago, and I wondered if that has stirred anything up for you."

Marla looked at Janet with her usual guarded expression. "I didn't like talking about that stuff, but I guess I probably have to if I'm going to get well."

"How are you feeling about your husband coming over for Family group tomorrow? Do you talk much during the week?"

"He calls me every day before he leaves the office and checks in with me. I guess I'm fine with him coming – maybe he'll learn something. It's hard though because he's not the greatest listener. He would rather talk!" Marla says with a smile.

"Marla, I noticed you were connecting pretty closely with Paul during group, and I wanted to point out it's very common for people in treatment to form close bonds. You live together 24 hours a day, so you start to feel like you've known each other a long time in a very short period of time. Sometimes we mix up intimacy with attraction. Have you noticed any strong feelings when you are with Paul?"

Marla looks embarrassed. "I'm married, Janet. I wouldn't do that to my husband, Gary. We were just making a silly joke out of something he drew—it's no more than that."

Janet looks at her quietly for a minute. "Marla, you're an attractive woman who has felt badly about yourself for a long time. As alcoholics, women are treated like they are a disappointment, like we're slutty or pathetic. Have you ever noticed how people talk about women who drink?"

Marla nods.

Janet continues. "What I'm concerned about is that you're in a vulnerable place right now, feeling crappy about yourself and your marriage. It would be very tempting to imagine a way to check out – run away from your current life and 'start over'. This is as true for Paul as it is for you. I am not suggesting that you and Paul are doing anything wrong at this point, at least not that I know of. I'm seeing you walk toward a cliff you may not know is there, and I'm serving as your warning light."

Marla looks like she is leaving her body. "What do you think about what I am saying to you?" Janet asks.

Marla focuses. "Honestly, I think you are over-reacting and jumping to conclusions. You're right that we haven't done anything wrong. However, (she sighs) I hear what you're saying, and it's true I forget my problems for a few minutes when Paul is telling me a silly story. It's been a long time since I laughed and it feels good." Marla added defensively.

"And I want you to laugh. I want you to feel alive again, Marla," Janet responds. "I also want you to look out for yourself and use your judgment when you are engaging with other people, even people here in treatment."

"Are you telling me that I can't talk to Paul anymore?" Marla asks.

"Not at all. There is no reason to do something that drastic. I just wanted to call your attention to what I'm seeing. You will decide what to do with the information." Janet reassured her.

"Okay then," Marla relaxes. "I'll pay better attention."

Janet smiles at her as Marla leaves the office. Ricardo walks by her on his way into the office. "Hey, just saw Marla. Everything okay?" he asks.

"I think it will be," Janet replies. "I wanted to call her attention to a little flirtation I saw her having with Paul during group. I think she'll be okay."

"I sure as shit hope so," Ricardo responds. "Her husband could become a nightmare, not to mention having to deal with Paul's fiancée!"

"Yea, I thought about that," Janet nods. "I think it's under control, but it's something for us to pay attention to. Where were you, anyway?"

"Oh, Angel had a court date. I took him over so I could stand in court with him and answer the judge's questions. It was pretty routine, they just wanted to make sure he was admitted and participating." Ricardo shares.

"Did you get a chance to talk to him about your call with his parole officer?" Janet wonders.

"Yea, I did. I let him know I was aware of the court dates and aware of the restraining order. He didn't say much other than, 'So, I guess you're not going to call her for me?' " Ricardo laughs. "These guys are scandalous! Of course I'm not going to call her and invite her over so she can violate the restraining order SHE took out!"

Janet giggles and remembers that she needs to touch bases with Kym before family day tomorrow just to pass on any concerns or heads up that might be helpful. It had been a long week, so she picks up the staff log to make sure she doesn't leave anything out and flips through the pages. She places the call and Kym answers, which rarely happens since she might be in class or with a client.

"Hey, girl, I am amazed I got you on the first try!" Janet says with a smile in her voice

"Hey, back. I'm on a class break, and saw it was you. I'm in research methods and I think I might staple my eyelids open…" Kym threatens.

Janet grins, "Well drastic times call for drastic measures! Speaking of which, I wanted to mention a couple of things for you to pay attention to tomorrow. I saw a flirtation between Marla and Paul during group today. I spoke with Marla about it, but I'm not sure if she will still be running that vibe with him tomorrow while her husband's here. Marla absolutely has to go to an SLE after treatment if she's going to have any hope of recovery. She acknowledges she drinks to tolerate sex with the guy, and they have had some violence between them. He's the money guy though, so we need his buy in. Can you meet with them as a couple?" Janet asks.

"Sure, no problem. We'll start the conversation now since we have some time before she completes. Who knows, he might even be relieved. Anything else?"

"Karen is in the hospital for tests—we called the paramedics when she fainted this morning. Her blood pressure meds need to be adjusted and they are making sure her meth use didn't create more heart damage. However, her parents might still be in family group. I'm not sure"

"I don't think I met Karen. She checked in on Sunday, right?" Kym confirms.

"Yea, that's right. I forgot about the timing. Paul is supposed to be working on being more grounded so he can work on being more present with his fiancée."

"So how does working Marla fit into this treatment plan?" Kym wonders.

"Come on. Dude doesn't even know he's doing it half the time. Read his autobiography if you have a minute. Oh, and Mark is graduating so you need to do the coin ceremony for him."

"That's right. Did he get an SLE placement?" Kym asks.

"Yes, his parole officer approved the non-licensed home yesterday. The house manager from that program will come and get him after family and transport him. The guy's name is Dave."

"Dave. Got it. Anything else?"

"Eddie is on medical leave, he was taking pills from the clients and the Clinical Director suggested he get medical leave and work on his recovery for a while. So, we're a little shorthanded. I'll be picking Karen up from the hospital when she's released, so I'll get to run into you. That's my reward for my good deed."

"Is Eddie okay? That must have been really hard. Good for the Clinical Director to handle it so kindly! The old guy surprises me sometimes."

"I think Eddie will be fine. Yea, sometimes the old guy's heart wakes up and says something," Janet jokes.

"By the way," Kym interrupts. "Do you think Carla's use in the facility will come up in family?"

"I don't really know. That seems so long ago – but it might. Oh, and one more thing. I keep meaning to ask Kevin's parents about his development. I swear he's delayed, LD, or has some sort of cognitive problem. If you get a chance, can you get a little more of his childhood history from them? He's not always the best self-reporter."

"I know what you mean. I'll try to make time." Kym promises.

"Oh, I almost forgot. What happened when you called Carolyn's husband? Is he going to bring the kids?"

"He is so worried, and so angry. I suggested that he leave the kids with his mother and come by himself so we can meet as a couple. Honestly, I think I need to refer him out for ongoing counseling," Kim notes, "He needs a lot of support."

"I think that's a great call. They have some serious work to do to salvage that marriage, and he needs as much help as she does. Thanks Kym. I know they're in good hands!" Janet offers.

"I appreciate the vote of confidence my friend. Oh, time for me to find the stapler. Class is starting!"

"Take Care," Janet says with a smile.

Ricardo was listening in on the run down for Kym. "It's amazing how much can happen in a week. The Carla-using thing seems a long time ago to me, too!"

"I know. There are so many of them, always in crisis. Thank God we do this as a team. There would be no other way to make it work." Janet observes.

SATURDAY

Kym arrives early to relieve Carl, who seems really subdued which puzzles her. They exchange a few words about the clients and he leaves. Even though she has her notes from Janet she takes a few minutes to read through the staff log anyway just to make sure.

Jesse arrives shortly after to assist her with greeting the visitors, making sure the visitor log is filled out and bags are searched. He watches the clients while Kym conducts the family-only group first. This group is a place for family members to ask questions about recovery, talk about their concerns and fears, and share some of their resentment that they are afraid to share with the addict because they are still so early in their recovery. Family is a term used loosely. It could consist of a close friend, siblings, children, grandparents, sponsors, significant others. The client gets to define the term family.

Kym can hear the clients setting up the chairs in the group room, nervously anticipating the arrival of family members. It's normal for several of the clients to have no support either because they're in treatment far away from home, or because they have asked everyone not to come... or they have burned so many bridges in their disease that no one wants to come. Regardless of the reason, it always makes Kym a little sad, so she is careful to sit next to or between people without family present to be surrogate family for that time.

She flips though the family program curriculum to determine her topic for the day. She provides some psychoeducation to the family, and then opens it up for general sharing. She keeps the psychoeducation fairly short, 20 minutes, to allow maximum time for them to talk to each other. It can be so comforting to hear that others have shared your struggle because addiction isolates family. People become secretive about the alcoholic and have shame in anticipation of people's judgment. If you're a parent, you agonize over what you may have done to "cause" them to turn to drugs. If you're a spouse, you struggle with what you can do to make them stop, and what you might be doing to make them drink. If you're a sibling you may be filled with worry or resentment over having your family taken hostage by addiction.

Kym decides on Communication Styles: Passive, Aggressive and Assertive. Family communication can become incredibly dysfunctional due to secrets, tantrums, guilting, accusations, and distrust. She decides to hand out a worksheet with examples of each type of communication style and ask them to add examples of their own. This encourages them to be more interactive.

Kym hears a quiet knock on the door and it is Carolyn. Kym remembers her from last admission as being critical, judging of the other clients, and controlling of her family. In fact, Kym remembers allowing the kids to bring their dog to help soothe them in their mother's angry presence. It was a hard family. She has suggested that Kym's husband NOT bring the children or the dog, and has planned to spend some time with the couple.

"Hi Kym. Do you remember me?" Carolyn asks hesitantly.

"Hi Carolyn, I surely do. I am sorry to see you here again, but I'm glad you're here in one piece. I know you talked to your husband and he has asked to meet with me as a couple, so your kids aren't coming. How are you doing with that?" Kym asks.

Carolyn looked on the verge of tears. "He's coming to serve me divorce papers, isn't he?" she asks.

Kym looks surprised, "No, honey. That's not the agenda at all! He wants to be able to talk to you without the kids so you can have an adult conversation. Because he's been so upset he feels he can keep better control of himself if someone else is there. Really."

Carolyn looked relieved. "I didn't sleep last night. I was so stressed out."

"Carolyn, my agenda is to talk to him about your depression and your treatment. I am hoping he will share his feelings and what he thinks he needs from you in recovery going forward.

The point of this conversation is to move forward." Kym gently touches Carolyn's arm in reassurance.

Carolyn left looking slightly less distressed and Kym found herself hoping for the best. "I hope to hell I haven't just lied to that woman," she thinks.

Kym heard Marla's husband, Gary, make an entrance. "He's so loud" Kym thought. "He takes up so much space!" Honestly she isn't looking forward to dealing with him. Controlling men really trigger her sometimes. They make her want to bully them back.

Kym

Kym started out as an alcohol and drug intern supervised by Janet, and now she's completing her master's degree as a Marriage and Family counselor. She is 37 years old, the mother of a 9 year old son with Aspergers. Kym was married to a Bipolar alcoholic for 15 years and ended the marriage after he refused to get treatment for either his Bipolar disorder or Alcoholism. The divorce was triggered by a child endangerment charge he picked up when he was pulled over for a DUI with their son in the backseat. He appeared disoriented and confused, and their son was hungry and frightened. Kym was called down to the police station and did not allow her husband to return to the home when he was released. He moved home to his parent's house.

Shortly after he moved out Kym noticed that their son, then 7 years old, seem to improve socially in school and in his behavior at home. He started being slightly less rigid and it was then that Kym understood that his father's erratic behavior had truly affected him. She placed him in play therapy and immediately enrolled in an alcohol and drugs studies program to learn more about addiction and how to treat it. She has pursued her studies hoping to become a licensed MFT and help other families navigate the disease that broke her heart and her family. Her husband, supervised by his parents, has visitation with their son on Saturdays allowing her to run the family program at the treatment center. Her ex-husband has largely stopped drinking but is still in denial about his Bipolar disorder. Every time he feels better he stops taking his medication which is a common trajectory for someone with Bipolar disorder. It can take up to ten years to accept the diagnosis. Unfortunately, when he is manic her ex-husband can be impatient and intolerant, bullying, demanding, and loud. Kym is aware of this and knows her reaction to Marla's husband is counter-transference. While anyone would be annoyed by him, she has an urge to slap him. So, she has talked about it in her own therapy and is hoping to be more objective.

Kym gathers her workbook and heads to the group room. On the way she is waylaid by Kevin's mother, Arlene, concerned that Kevin has been complaining he's not sleeping well, even on the suboxone. She wonders if she should ask her physician for a few Ambien, about a week's worth, to help him through. Kym just looks at her for a moment, and remembers Janet's request to learn more about Kevin's development. Listening to his mom, Kym can't help but wonder about Arlene's development. Who puts their kid in rehab for prescription med's then suggests bringing in MORE pills to help him? Pills not even prescribed to *him,* but through *her own* doctor?! This leads Kym to believe that whatever might be going on with Kevin is possibly genetic.

Kym tactfully suggests to Kevin's mom that offering more pills could undermine their attempt to encourage him to use alternative approaches to relaxation such as meditation and exercise. Arlene nods in agreement and drops the topic. Kym shakes her head as she follows Arlene into group.

Family Group

Kym takes her place at the front of the room after greeting each of the family members. It's not a large group today: Paul's fiancée; Amanda's boyfriend; Carolyn's husband, Frank; Angel's mom and sister; Karen's parents; Marla's husband; Kevin's parents; and Laura's parents. Even though Mark is graduating today, he does not have family present.

Kym opens the group with her focus on communication styles as she has planned, and the families seem to quickly recognize their own style, as well as the addict or alcoholic's style. In fact, typical of family they were far more focused on the addict and alcoholic than themselves, so she had to keep gently re-directing them back toward recognizing their own communication patterns and how they affected their relationship with the addict in their lives. It was easy to point to the addict/alcoholic's contribution to the family chaos, but family members could be just as chaotic; sometimes even worse!

Pauls' fiancée, Joyce, helped open the group to general discussion with an observation, "I know I should probably be more direct with Paul, or assertive as you are saying, but I am afraid he will get mad and shut down. Once he does that, I have to wait until HE'S ready to talk and that could be a couple of days. I get so anxious when he checks out, so worried he's going to drink, that it's easier for me to just keep my mouth shut"

"But is it easier?" Laura's mom, Kate, asks "Because I do that too, and things build up and build up then I find myself screaming so I look like the crazy woman and my loaded daughter looks saner than I do!"

Carolyn's husband, Frank, was nodding. "I spend so much energy trying to keep her okay so she won't get angry or have an excuse to drink. It never works. When my wife was here last time she spent the whole time complaining about everyone else, including me. Sometimes I've wondered if maybe I am the reason she drinks and maybe she'd be better off married to someone else?"

Marla's husband Gary jumps in, "I don't get that. You sound a lot like me, Frank. We do everything for our wives. Provide a beautiful house, all the money they need, great vacations, nice kids. What do they have to complain about? I don't see why Marla needs to drink. Other women would kill to be in her shoes! Instead she's quiet, never says anything, and always looks a little miserable. I think she just needs to pull her head out of her ass!"

Everyone looks vaguely shocked by this statement, and Kym steps in. "Gary, I'm hearing a lot of resentment and blame, and I wonder if you talk to Marla like this? It may be why she shuts down around you. On the other hand, I also hear that you are genuinely puzzled and would like to help her."

"Of course I want to help her! That's why I put her in this place. I want to get the woman I married back – can you do that?"

"What I can do is help Marla try to find a way back to herself so she can make better decisions and be clearer about what she needs and wants. I am hoping to spend some time with the two of you to talk about that. Are you willing?" Kym challenges.

Gary thinks a minute. "I will do whatever it takes," he says surprisingly softly.

Kym finds herself feeling a glimmer of compassion for the guy. He was clearly feeling a loss of control and was frightened about how far away Marla has become. "*Maybe there's hope,*" she thinks to herself.

Angel's mother, Manuela, raises her hand indicating she has a question. "I'm worried not just about Angel's drug use, but that he'll go back to prison. Last time he was out, he was using drugs, and he abused my grand baby's mother. It's probably my fault," she says with tears in her eyes. "His father was wild like Angel, and would hit me sometimes in front of the children." Her daughter takes Manuela's hand.

"He got arrested last time for showing up at her house and pounding on the door. He was threatening to kill her if she didn't let him in. He was screaming and hollering, and she called 911 so the operator heard the whole thing. He went to jail for violating his restraining order and some kind of threat."

"You mean terrorist threat?" Kym asks.

She nodded. "Yes, that's it. I am afraid if he doesn't stay clean my grandson will never know his father," she says as the tears are rolling down her cheeks.

The room was quiet.

"It is such a powerless feeling, isn't it? Being unable to prevent people you love from making terrible decisions?" Kym says gently.

"Can anyone else relate to Manuela's powerlessness?" Kym prompts.

"I don't understand why they don't just quit?" Angel's sister asks. "Can't they see the damage they are causing in their lives?"

"Last week we talked about it being a disease, and looked at the biology of it." Kym points to the *Neurobiology of Addiction* poster behind her. "I know it is hard to see because it looks like they are choosing to drink and use. I mean you can't get drunk without taking a drink, right?"

Everyone nods.

She moves over to the poster and points at the parts of the brain as she speaks. "However, once the neurochemistry of an addict changes and their tolerance grows, the fear of the illness of withdrawal begins to haunt them. They need increasing amounts of drugs and alcohol to feel biochemically 'normal' and to avoid the sickness that follows when it leaves their system. Their frontal lobe ability to plan, organize their thoughts, follow through, and manage impulses becomes hijacked by their mid-brain and they begin to operate at the mercy of the relentless craving system. Life become suspended as they organize their existence around getting and using the drug that drives them. By the time they are addicted they are no longer chasing the high – they are avoiding the pain of craving."

"So, when Karen is using meth she is trying to feel "normal" and not have cravings? She is not just partying and having fun?" Karen's mother, Jean, asks.

"I know it starts out like that. And people always think they will be able to handle it - use every now and then. And it takes over their lives. Even when they start to go to jail or fight with their family, they can't seem to stop. It's scary to lose control so they tell themselves they don't WANT to stop. The truth is they can't without feeling withdrawal."

Carolyn's husband Frank jumps in, "She's constantly telling me she can handle the alcohol; she can quit whenever she wants to.

Carolyn acts like it's a choice."

Kym nodded. "That's called denial. They lie to themselves before they ever lie to us. You know how powerless you feel when you can't make her stop drinking?"

Frank nods.

"She feels that powerless when she tries to stop drinking on her own. She can't believe she can't 'control' a beverage – for God's sake!" Janet explains.

Everyone smiles

"Trust and know that they get scared when they finally admit to themselves they are out of control."

"So we both feel out of control of alcohol?" Frank asks.

"Exactly! That's why we refer you to Alanon to learn to deal with your feelings of powerlessness, and AA for Carolyn to learn to deal with hers. You have more in common than you think." Kym adds.

After a few minutes Kym closes the group, while everyone takes a break before the large group meeting.

Kym checks in with Jesse as the family's mill around greeting their family members. Some of them get a cup of coffee or a donut; and some need a smoke. Kym finds the coin they used in completion ceremonies at the treatment program. The ritual is to pass the coin around the circle with each member putting some positive energy into the coin. The graduate then keeps the coin in his/her pocket as a reminder of that positive energy. Since Mike didn't have any family, Kym would lead off the ceremony.

Multi-Family Group

The family and clients re-enter the group room creating a much larger group. It is a chance for Kym to observe the clients with their family members, and get a read on body language. 70% of communication is unspoken, so those cues are important. Kym welcomes everyone and has them go around the room introducing themselves and stating why they are there. Many of the family members had been there last week, so only Angel's mother and sister, and Carolyn's husband Frank were new.

Kym decides to present Virginia Satir's Process of Change to normalize the struggle for the families. It is important to her that the families identify with change themselves, and not just be thinking about what the client's need to do. She drew the following chart:

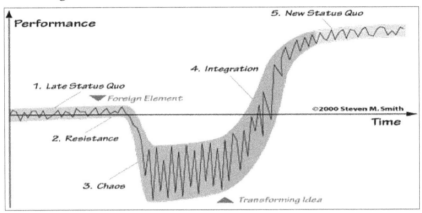

Kym then moves through each stage of the process, emphasizing that changing anything is difficult, and it usually takes the introduction of a foreign element, like a boss or a judge or a crisis to force us to consider change. No matter how hard something is, it is familiar. It's the devil we know.

She emphasizes that the chaos during the adjustment, working toward a new status quo, is chaotic and uncomfortable. Even when families have desperately wanted recovery, the actuality of the time away from the family, the ongoing meetings and support groups, the changes in communication and participation levels are disruptive. Many families panic, and run back to the old normal. The key is to move into integration, where they keep practicing new skills until they have a "new" status quo that feels normal to them.

Members of the group are invited to share where they are currently in the process of change, and times when they have been successful or unsuccessful in changing something that mattered to them. It did not have to be alcohol or drug related.

Most people can relate to the ambivalence of change, and hands started going up all over the room.

Kym can see that Laura's mother, Kate, is having a hard time with this concept, and Kym sees her raise her hand.

"Yes, Kate. What's going on?"

"Can I ask Mike a question?" she asks Kym.

"You need to ask Mike," Kym encourages her.

"Mike, can I ask you a question about your using?"

"Sure," he says tentatively.

"I understand why we fight change, because it makes us uncomfortable. But you had so MANY consequences. How could that have been more comfortable for you than quitting?"

Kym is always happy when this happens. Family members tend to listen to addicts differently than their own family members because they have some objectivity. Kym also knows Mike can handle it.

"Well, you're right. You would think that DUI's, possession arrests, and losing my wife would be enough. When I look at it sober, it seems amazing that it took me so long! I don't know how it is for other people, but what happened for me was that I made a huge mistake early in my life and went to jail. It's like I never recovered from that—I couldn't forgive myself and would drink to forget. I would use to forget. As the mistakes piled up it seemed like the hole was bigger and bigger and it was too late to get out."

"So how did you get out?" Kate asks.

"Weirdly enough I ran into an old high school buddy who remembered me. I had been a quarterback, and a good student. He just assumed I was successful. As we talked I started to remember that I was smart once; I was strong once. Then he told me he had been sober for five years, and suggested we go to a meeting. I didn't go right then but when I was released this time, I remembered the conversation and since I already had some clean time in jail, I decided to stay clean and see what happens."

Kate looks at Laura, "Have you ever felt like it was too late to start over? Like you had made too many mistakes?"

Laura smiles at her mother. "Absolutely. Fortunately, YOU never thought it was too late, and you and dad kept trying to help me even when I stopped trying to help myself. Without you, I would probably be dead."

Kate hugged Laura, while the rest of the room watched quietly, some with tears in their eyes.

"This seems like a good time for Mike's graduation ceremony," Kym announces. She pulls the coin out from her skirt pocket.

"Mike, I've watched you get taller and taller; you were wilted when you came in and now your stalk is stronger. I am so impressed with the wisdom you carry, and I can see the high school guy you referred to as you were talking. You're still in there. I wish you well, and hold great hope for you."

Kym smiles, then passes the coin around the circle, each person sharing an observation about Mike, something they learned from him, or simply wishing him well. It was obvious he was moved by the session, and comments on how warm the metal coin is in his front pocket.

The group closes with the Serenity Prayer, and the group breaks out with family groupings and client groupings moving toward the kitchen for lunch. Angel's mother brought him enchiladas, and invites Mike to join them before his ride comes to take him to the SLE.

As Kym is gathering her papers she notices Laura's mother hug Mike, which warms Kym's heart. "*I love what I do,*" she thinks for the thousandth time.

She is going to meet with Carolyn and Frank after lunch, so

she heads into the office to eat while charting the session. Janet arrives as Kym is typing, having returned with Karen from the hospital. Janet is pensive as she sits at her desk, and Kym asks her about the pick-up. Janet thinks back, while she relates the story to Kym.

Karen

"Hey, girl. You look better today" Janet observes as Karen gets in the car. *"What did the doctor say?"*

"He says I'm going to be okay, especially if I stay off the meth," she laughs. "But I also got some other news."

"What's that?" Janet asks.

"It looks like I am pregnant." Karen says quietly.

"How far along are you?" Janet wonders.

"I'm about 4-5 weeks they think. They wanted to know what I want to do about the pregnancy since I was using meth during the first weeks. The baby could be fine, or not okay. It's hard to know."

"What do you want to do?" Janet asks.

"I'm not sure. I split up with my boyfriend 3 weeks ago before he got arrested. I don't have a job, and I may have hurt the baby… but I don't believe in abortion, and I have always wanted a kid. I'm confused right now."

"Well I can see why you would be." Janet says. "You don't have to decide right now, you have a window of time to think about it, talk it over with your family, or maybe write about it in your journal. Have you ever been pregnant before?"

"One other time, and I had an abortion and I felt so guilty. I still feel guilty. I am afraid if I have another one God will never let me get pregnant again to punish me. Is that silly?"

"I don't think it's silly. I don't see God quite as punishing, but I can see why you would want to take your time to think this through. It's a maternal decision, really." Janet adds.

"What do you mean, maternal?"

"Well, you're making a decision about what's best for your baby. That's what mothers do. Sometimes the best decision is to keep the child, other times it's to have the child and place her in a stable home, and sometimes it's best not to let her be born at all."

"Why do you keep saying her?"

"I guess because I'm remembering a very hard time in my life many years ago. It is one of the hardest decisions you will make, and I'm so glad you are sober."

"So you aren't judging me? I'm afraid my parents will be so mad at me for being so irresponsible. They don't know about the other abortion."

"Maybe it's better to get your thoughts sorted out before talking to them so you can approach them from a position of strength rather than guilt or shame. What do you think?"

"I think you might be right. I don't think I'll tell them yet." Karen agrees.

"Did they send you home with prenatal vitamins?" Janet asks. *"I'll check them in when we get to the center."*

Kym asked Janet what is troubling her about the encounter.

"It brings up my miscarriage years ago, which was an act of God at the time. I had no business with a kid at that point in my life. But I still get sad about it every now and then, especially now that I am waaay too long in the tooth to have one now!" she smiles.

"What do you think Karen will do?" Kym wonders.

"It's so hard. In all honestly, she doesn't have any way to support the child and emotionally she's a mess. On the other hand, some women use having a child as a reason to get and stay sober - their maternal instinct kicks in and they make some life changes. I suppose it has to do with her support system. She isn't too sure her parents are going to be with her on this, and I don't see her doing it without them."

"And the father?" Kym asks.

"He's locked up at the moment. They broke up before he went to jail so she doesn't see a future for them as a family."

"So she really must feel alone." Kym says.

"Yes, I imagine she does. So we will have to be her family for now. Maybe the other women, including Amanda, can help her with the decision. They know the reality of mothering in recovery. I have to trust the group process."

Kym nods. "You're right, there are some strong women in here with a lot of life experience. She'll get what she needs."

"In the meantime, I will lock up her prenatal meds and her new blood pressure medicine with the rest of the medicine, and put them in the med log." Janet says as she is writing.

Jesse pokes his head in the room. "Hi Janet. I saw Karen. Is there anything I need to know about her med's?" he asks.

"She has a new dosage. And she has prenatal vitamins she needs to take," Janet adds.

"Whoa. How does she feel about it? She looks kind of spacey talking to her parents. Pretty shut down."

"She doesn't want to tell them until she makes a decision, so she's probably finding the conversation hard."

"Mike's ride, Dave, is here to pick him up. Did he sign out and get his medication?"

Janet checks his chart. "Yes, his discharge is signed, and here are his meds. Thanks a lot, Jesse."

"You are most welcome," he grins as he leaves.

"What are you going to do with the rest of your afternoon?" Kym asks Janet.

Welcome To My World

"I haven't thought about it, really. Maybe go see a movie then catch a meeting with my sponsor."

"Are you ever going to date again?" Kym asks pointedly. "You deserve a life you know."

"So I'm told. The truth is even though I know he never loved me, and is living happily with the bimbo who's popping out his babies, I'm not over him. Honestly, I'm scared I never will be." Janet says quietly.

"Are you ever going to call her anything but the Bimbo?"

"Sometimes I say skank or mouth breather. Why?"

Kym just laughed. "Bitter, party of one!" she teases.

"Indeed," Janet laughs. "Guilty as charged."

As Janet leaves the room, Carolyn and Frank poke their heads in. "Is this a good time?" Frank asks.

"This is the perfect time," Kym says as she offers them chairs. "How was your lunch? Did you find anything to talk about?" Kym smiles.

"I told Carolyn what we talked about in the family group, how she may feel just as out of control with alcohol as I feel about her drinking. I never thought about it like that."

"Do you feel out of control?" Kym asks Carolyn.

"I do this time. I feel like my life is slipping away from me, and I am going to lose everything. At the same time, I still wish I could drink because these feelings would go away for a while. When I think about the way I feel, and never having a break, it seems too hard for me."

Frank asks Carolyn, "What are you feeling that seems so hard? Is it the marriage, the kids? What's making you so unhappy that you have to drink?"

"No, honey. It's not you and the kids. I was talking to Janet and I think it may be depression, she suggested postpartum

98

depression. I have never been fully okay since Trish was born, and I keep trying to hide it. I know you can feel I am not "all there" sometimes, and I've been afraid you would judge me as a bad mother."

Frank looks at Kym. "Is the depression something you guys can help her with? Should she see our family doctor? I thought depression meant that you were sad all the time." Frank looks at Carolyn, "No offense honey, but most of the time you looked mad to me."

Kym offers, "Sometimes depression can look flat, sometimes it is agitated, or angry depression. In Carolyn's case she was fighting her fatigue and difficulty concentrating, and probably used anger to give her enough energy to cope. Then she drank to take the edge off. It's a very bad cycle. In answer to your question, yes we would like her to see a Psychiatrist. If you don't have one on your insurance panel that you want to use, we can refer you to our guy."

Kym looks at Frank, "What do you need from Carolyn to feel like she's committed to her recovery. It may take you awhile to fully trust it; that would be natural."

"I think I need her to take her alcoholism seriously. I have had a hard time concentrating at work when she has been drinking, worrying about the children and worrying about her driving. I am worried about the legal bills from her DUI and paying for her driver's classes. But I can make all of that work if I know she's taking her recovery seriously."

"How would you know I'm serious?" Carolyn asks.

"You would go to the doctor; go to your Drivers classes regularly and not miss; you would go to your AA meetings and get a sponsor; you would go to Outpatient treatment after residential. Last time you refused to do anything they recommended. It really tanked quickly."

"You're right. I fought the whole thing last time. I felt picked on, and I was a pain in the ass! I'm lucky they were willing to have me back." Carolyn smiles. "I promise I will take direction this time. I think the depression thing plays a big part and now that I'm admitting it, I have more hope even if I feel like crap."

Kym offers, "I think we can help get you to the doctor and help you feel less crappy."

Kym talks to the couple for a few more minutes until they were ready to close and they go back outside for a cup of coffee and talk about the kids.

Kym wanders outside to check in on the families, and sees them talking together fairly well. Jesse was right, Karen does look shut down. She spies Marla and Gary sitting outside in the swing, and it looks tense. She heads over to them, and asks if this might be a good time for them to meet?

"We might as well," Gary says. "She's not talking to me here, so maybe having you with us will help."

Marla nods in agreement, and the three of them head into the office. Once everyone was seated, Kym asks Marla directly,

"Marla, Gary is obviously under the impression that you don't want to talk to him. Is he right?"

Marla thinks a minute. "I never know what to say to him. As soon as I start to tell him what I am thinking he starts giving me advice, or telling me I am being ridiculous. I figure there is no point in saying anything since he treats me like a moron."

Gary is defensive, "I do not say you are a moron! When I give you my two cents it is only because I want to help you make your life easier. I just want you to be happy, and I can never seem to make you happy. I can't do anything right!"

"You want me to be happy so I will have sex with you! You don't give a shit if I am happy otherwise. My job is to keep your house clean, take care of your kids, and put out when you want it. I don't even exist!" Marla shouts.

Kym thinks to herself, *"Well there you are! You've been playing possum. Now I can picture the shoving and slapping."*

Gary looks wounded.

Kym intervenes. "Okay, you obviously have a lot to say to each other that you've been sitting on. There's no need to air all of it at one time. I'm wondering if 30 days residential is going to be enough time for you to be ready to go back home, Marla."

"What do you mean?" Gary asks, "The program is only 30 days. Shouldn't that be enough time for her to figure out what's going on with her? We need her at home!" Gary explains to Kym.

Kym can see Marla wince.

"Gary, do you need Marla at home or do you miss her?"

"Well of course I miss her, dammit! Isn't that what I just said?"

"Well, the way you delivered the message left out the part about how you were feeling. It actually sounded pretty judgmental – like she should get her shit together and go home to do her job."

"You sound like her now," Gary says obviously offended. Kym had to think about this a minute, because she knows Gary pushes her buttons.

"Gary, I didn't mean to offend you. I am sorry if it sounded like I was judging you!"

Gary nodded. "What did you mean about more time?"

"Did you mean a Sober Living Environment (SLE)?" Marla asks.

"Sometimes people need more time to heal before they return home. Living in a SLE while doing the Outpatient program would allow you to take care of the household and children, while still giving you time for your meetings and Outpatient. You would have a 9:00 p.m. curfew during the week, and 11:00 p.m. on the weekends so you would have a safe place to return to regroup and have the support of other women."

"How much Is this SLE?" Gary asks.

"It is about $700.00 a month and you provide your own food. You would go to four meetings a week plus your Outpatient, you would have chores like you do here, and there would be random drug testing and house meetings a few times a week to check in. So there is structure but much more freedom during the day."

"I don't know," Gary says hesitantly. "How much longer would she be gone?"

"Gary, what is the hardest part for you about having me gone?" Marla asks.

"I don't like being alone with the kids. The house doesn't feel right without you. You're what makes the house feel like a home," he says.

Marla looked at him quietly for a minute. "Am I really different when I'm drunk? Do the kids notice?"

Gary smiled at her, "Honey, it's pretty obvious. You repeat yourself, you don't remember what we tell you, and you fall asleep early on the couch. Sometimes while we're talking to you! It's like you disappear."

"So even if Marla spent less time at home but was awake and responsive when she was there, it would still be a lot more connection than you've been having, right?" Kym asks.

Gary thinks a minute. "You're probably right. It would be nice for her to really be with us, like she is right now… I think we could make this SLE thing work if you think it's best for her," Gary says to Kym.

"Well, we can talk more about it as time gets closer, but I thought it would be good to go ahead and put it out there so you can consider it." Kym clarifies. "You guys are doing a great job sitting here – I know this isn't easy. Why don't you go back outside and talk about something neutral for a little while – maybe the kids?" Kym suggests.

They nod and head back out to the swing. Kym takes a deep breath, and rolls her neck which had started to tense.

Raul

They pass Jesse who was watching Raul. Raul has been sitting by himself chain smoking since group ended. Jesse joins him, "Hey, Raul man. What's going on?"

Raul barely glances at him.

"You've been sitting here for a while now. Do you want some lunch?" Jesse asks.

"Not hungry."

"Is it hard being here without your family?"

"I should be seeing MY son. The bitch didn't call me even though I wrote her," he says angrily.

"That must hurt," Jesse observes.

"It doesn't hurt, man. It pisses me off!" he says with force.

"Okay. I got it. What's going through your mind right now?"

"I don't know. Just thinking."

"Well, if it were me I'd be thinking about how I am going to find her."

Raul looks at him, "Yeah?"

"Yeah. Then I would have to think about whether or not it would be worth me doing a few more minutes when I get rolled up."

Raul sits quietly. "But a man should see his son. How will he know who I am?" Raul says still heated.

"What kind of guy was your dad?" Jesse asks.

"My dad? My dad worked a lot. There were 8 of us, and my mom cleaned houses when she wasn't taking care of us."

"Did your dad drink?"

"Yeah, all the men did. They would do what they had to do for the families, and take a break on the weekend."

"Did your dad ever do time?"

"Why you talkin' about my dad, man?"

"Because being a dad seems to mean something to you, so I wondered if it was because you felt a lot for your own dad."

Raul thought about this. "I didn't have a lot of time with him – he was always busy working. Maybe I wish it was different with my own boy?" Raul suggests.

Jess nods. "It would make sense. You know the lasagna's gonna run out if you don't get your issue. I'd get a plate if I were you."

Raul nods, and walks toward the house.

Jesse

Jesse sat and thought about his own dad for a minute. Jesse's parents own their own machine shop. His mother does the books and his dad works in the shop. His parents worked long hours to make money to support Jesse and his two sisters, and even though he was able to play school sports, his parents rarely had time to attend. In their minds, providing him the opportunity was the support he needed, and they didn't realize how much he wished they had been there. He never wanted them to feel guilty by bringing it up. Jesse's dad also drank at night to wind down and deal with his financial insecurity as the business was often affected by the economy. When times were good his dad could hire more help and be around a little more. When times were hard he did much more of the work himself. Jesse doesn't know how much his relationship with his dad has affected him, though he knows his dad loves him. He just doesn't really "know" his dad. His dad is cut from old school cloth, so they usually talk about sports, current events, his sisters. Nothing very personal like the conversations he has with his sponsor. "Maybe someday" he thinks as he sees movement out of the corner of his eye.

"That looks like Amanda," he thinks as he gets up to investigate.

Sure enough, Amanda and her boyfriend are on the side of the building, and as Jesse rounds the corner Amanda's boyfriend

Todd is zipping his pants. They both look surprised, and Amanda turns pink.

"So guys," Jesse begins.

"Dude," Todd interrupts. "I know it was wrong. It was my idea."

Amanda joins in, "I know we shouldn't have. I am soooo embarrassed." She looks like she's going to cry.

"Todd, I have to ask you to leave right now. I'll have to talk to the team about what they want to do at Clinical Staffing on Monday."

Todd nods, and goes inside to get his backpack.

Todd looks at Amanda. "It's not the end of the world – just against the rules. You're putting your reunification with your daughter at risk when you do this stuff. "

Amanda nods with tears in her eyes. "I know, I know. I just do things sometimes without thinking. Maybe I don't deserve to get my daughter back," she cries.

Jesse smiled. "I'm not the sex police, and I'm not here to judge you. But I would suggest that you talk with Janet on Monday about how to handle yourself better so you make better decisions. We're a work in progress, girl. Not perfection."

Amanda nods and heads to the front to say goodbye to Todd.

"I need a frigging cigarette" Jesse thinks as he sits in the smoking area. *"I probably also need to get laid"* he thinks to himself and grins.

Close to 3:00 p.m. Jesse starts to gather up the remaining family members to usher them out for the day. Kym is finished with her shift and Jorge arrives to relieve her. Phone privileges start at 4:00, and the clients will read, do laundry, sleep, exercise, or watch T.V. for the afternoon until their inside meeting at 6:30. Tonight H&I (Hospitals and Institutions) are coming from NA so it will be a speaker meeting.

Jesse heads in to the office to make some notes in the log about Raul and Amanda. Since he is not a primary counselor, he will let the counselors decide how to handle the situation on Monday. He looks forward to being a primary counselor, and enjoyed talking with Raul today. He could also see how his own stuff can get stirred up, which must be that counter-transference thing his teachers talk about.

The Clinical Director has hired Sarah as a CD tech in Eddie's absence, and this will be her first shift on her own. Jesse figures he'll hang out for a while to make sure she's okay, and then take-off for a 7:30 meeting. *"She's a nice girl,"* he thinks to himself. *"Too bad she's married."*

Jesse hears a quiet knock on the door and it's Kevin.

"Hey Jesse. Sorry to bother you" Kevin begins.

"It's no bother, bro. What do you need?"

"I was talking to my mom and she thinks I may need something stronger to sleep than Unison and the Suboxone I am taking. I really worry about getting enough sleep because I read it can make you sick. It may even make you psychotic, like the way they torture prisoners of war is to not let them sleep. How would I know I am getting psychotic because of sleep?" Kevin worries.

Jesse stares at him for a few seconds. "Kevin, I checked the log when I came in, and Carl said you were sleeping every time he did bed check."

"I only looks like I'm sleeping. I'm just lying there trying to sleep," Kevin counters.

"Tell me about your bedtime routine," Jesse asks.

"Well I stop watching TV and read my Big Book until I get tired. Then I go outside and have a cigarette, then come in and pee and go to bed."

"There's your problem," Jesse points out. "Cigarettes have a stimulant in them. They wake you up, so it makes it hard for you to sleep. You have to stop smoking earlier in the evening to get better rest."

"Do you really think it would make a difference?" Kevin asks anxiously. "I think my mom may be right."

"Let's give it a try for a few days and see. I promise you are getting enough sleep to not be psychotic," Jesse smiles.

Kevin smiles back, and heads outside for a smoke. People smoke way more in rehab. In fact, some people take up smoking in rehab as a cross-addiction, which is frustrating to the non–smoking staff! All the research indicates that smokers have a higher relapse rate. Your best bet is to quit everything at once and let your extra dopamine receptors close down. But recovery culture states that smoking is better than drinking and crack, and it isn't possible to quit everything at once. Instead it's like the layers of an onion, quitting one thing at a time. However, both founders of AA died from nicotine-related illness so it's an ongoing dilemma.

Jesse is still chuckling to himself when Sarah arrives for her shift. She's nervous about being left alone, but also excited about the challenge. She is relieved to see Jesse. Jesse encourages her to read the log book to get oriented.

Jesse sees Sarah's eyebrows raise about Amanda, and he encourages her to share her thoughts.

"I was thinking that maybe I could talk to her later about managing her impulses through mindfulness. I just completed a 2-day training, and I learned some cool skills."

"Anything you can give her will help, I'm sure," Jesse says. "She really needs to get this before reunification happens," Jesse points out.

Sarah nods. "I'll see what I can do… it looks like you did a good job with Raul. I am a little worried about him. He always feels like a powder keg to me. He makes me nervous, actually." Sarah admits.

"I did time with guys like that," Jesse says. "They have a strong rigid set of beliefs about how other people should act, even if the rules don't apply to them. They can get offended pretty easily, and be surprisingly conservative in their thinking and politics. It's interesting really," Jesse explains.

Sarah looks like she is thinking. "By the way, what time does H&I get here? I am looking forward to the NA meeting because I normally attend AA. It has a different feel to it."

Jesse nods in agreement. "Yeah, the opening is a little different and we close with Just for Today. My friend Mike is speaking, so I think the group is in for a good meeting."

"I think I'll go wander around the house now and see what everyone is up to. Are you going to get the med's ready? I'm not very comfortable doing that." Sarah asks.

"No problem. I got to ask the Clinical Director a couple of clarifying questions this week, so I feel comfortable."

"Okay, I think I'll wander around and see what everyone is doing," she says as she leaves.

The H&I speaker, Mike, arrives at 6:15, and Jesse can hear the clients setting up the group room anticipating the meeting. Jesse gives Mike a hug and offers him some tea or water. Mike checks in to see if the house needs a particular topic, and they banter some ideas around. Jesse was thinking of self-care for Raul and suggests, "To thine own self be true," a recovery slogan. Jesse then gestures to Sarah that he's taking off and she waves good bye across the room.

Because it is an in-house meeting, the meeting format is shifted a little, though it's set up to be a full meeting experience. One of the residents will function as the secretary and follow the format, which is an opening and some readings. No one reads the secretary report or seventh tradition.

Tonight's secretary will be Angel, who reads from the script:

Hello, I'm an addict and my name is Angel. Welcome to the Recovery home group of Narcotics Anonymous. We will open this meeting with a moment of silence for the addict who still suffers, followed by the **WE** version of the Serenity Prayer.

Is there anyone here attending their first NA meeting, or this meeting for the first time? If so, WELCOME! You are the most important people here!

There is one 'must' that applies to everyone attending, that no drugs or paraphernalia be on your person at meetings. If you are carrying anything please take it outside and leave it, then you are welcome back in. This is for the protection of the meeting place and the NA fellowship as a whole. If you've used today, please listen to what is being said and talk to someone at the break or after the meeting. It costs nothing to belong to this fellowship; you are a member when you say you are. (This always causes the residential clients to smile and poke each other)

Could someone please read:

1) Who is an addict — Amanda steps up.

2) What is the NA Program — Paul steps up.

3) Why are we here — Laura steps up.

4) How it works — Kevin steps up.

5) The Twelve Traditions of NA — Carolyn steps up.

Angel continues, "I'd like to introduce tonight's speaker, Mike, who will share for 20 minutes then open the meeting up to the group."

Mike smiles and begins with how it was, and quickly moves to how it is now and how he uses the program to stay clean even though he has 10 years. He announces he will remain after the meeting for a while if anyone needs to talk, and clients have an opportunity to share. This is important practice for new people who have a chance to learn meeting format and culture. Many people in recovery have never been listened to, and the lack of feedback allows them the space to hear themselves without worrying about another person's response. Lack of cross-talk can be really freeing.

As the meeting breaks up, Mike thanks Angel who looks a little embarrassed, and Karen approaches him to learn more about sponsorship. In fact, she asks if he can sponsor her because she needs one for her court requirements. Mike explains that men don't sponsor women, and that at her next outside meeting he should put her name in the sponsor box and a woman will call her. Karen seems disappointed by this and asks him if she can have his number anyway, "Just to talk."

Mike smiles at her and tells her that when people are new they are pretty vulnerable, and that the women should stick to the women so things don't get "complicated." He gives her a "recovery hug" and turns to talk to Paul.

Sarah is watching this exchange and thinks to herself, *"Good for him!"* Not everyone in recovery is this honest or respectful, and "thirteenth stepping" is rampant. This is when someone with a lot of clean time starts dating a newcomer who quickly makes the new relationship their focus instead of their recovery.

Karen

Sarah lets Jorge know she is going to follow Karen out to the smoking area, wondering how she is handling what she could easily see as a rejection.

"Hey Karen," Sarah calls as she heads to the chair next to Karen.

"I saw what happened in there. Are you okay?"

Karen looks deflated. "I feel like I just got dumped even though I didn't even know the guy. Do I look that desperate?" she asks as she flicks her cigarette.

"I can see why you'd feel that way. And it's not like that – Mike was doing what he's supposed to do."

"What's that, piss women off?" Karen says with annoyance. "He acts like I was offering to blow him."

Sarah laughs. "Actually, you may have gotten a different response if you did! No seriously, everyone newly in recovery is vulnerable. Everyone wants to feel better, and a new relationship is a natural choice – a natural high, right?" Sarah asks.

"I guess so. Maybe I did think he was a little hot." Karen admits.

"Well that's 'cause he is," Sarah agrees. "How are you feeling? I noticed the prenatal vitamins in the med log."

"I feel okay, just really confused. I had this dream last night that the baby's father, Brent, called and told me he was going to be released early and we were going to be a family... I know it's a dream. We broke up before he went to jail, so it would never happen," she says sadly.

"Why did you split up?" Sara asks.

"We were both out of control; fighting all the time. I got tired of it, so I left."

"Do you think the fighting was drug-related?"

"Probably, we were both gacked out most of the time. But even when we were clean, which was rare, we still fought when we tried to make decisions. It's like we were fighting about control most of the time. And he could get really mean."

"So even if your dream came true, it would be hard to have a family with him?" Sarah prompts.

Karen thought for a minute. "Honestly, I don't think he's ever had a legit job—he was always a dealer. I'm not sure he could support us unless he worked under the table somewhere."

"That sounds dicey"

"Yeah, it would be," Karen sighs. They were both quiet for a while, listening to the crickets.

"How would you support the baby if it was just you?" Sarah asks.

"Well I've been thinking I could get food stamps and health care through the county. Maybe I could get financial aid to go to school to learn how to do something that would make decent money."

"Who would watch the baby while you were in classes?"

"That's the problem. I am not sure my parents would help me, and all my friends are users like me."

"You might qualify for subsidized childcare through Tanif," Sarah offers.

"My real worry is that I was using when I was pregnant. I didn't even know I was pregnant! So, I may have already hurt the baby. Is it fair to bring a baby into the world to deal with whatever problems it's going to have because of MY mistake? It doesn't seem right somehow."

Sarah sat quietly knowing there was no real answer to this question.

"It seems to me that you don't have all the information," Sarah observes. "Until you see a doctor and see what they can tell you about possible damage to your baby, and until you talk to your parents about childcare, you would have a hard time deciding."

Karen nodded at this. "I guess I need to work up the courage to do both. I need to schedule an OB/GYN appointment and talk to my parents."

"You have some time to get this done. How far along are you?"

"They guessed 4 or 5 weeks."

"Okay, you can call and schedule with the doctor on Monday and talk to Janet in your one-on-one about approaching your parents. You might even be able to meet with Kym and your parents next Saturday to have some support," Sarah suggests.

Karen looks relieved to have a plan. "Thanks, Sarah. I feel a little more focused now. Thanks for following me out here."

"You're welcome! Let's go in and see if we can wrestle the remote from Kevin," Sarah laughs.

SUNDAY

Jesse and Keisha relieved Carl the next morning, who is acting more like his usual 'Tigger' self. Jesse is in charge of "double scrub" that morning. This is the treatment program ritual during which the clients clean the recovery home thoroughly. They clean the refrigerator, clean the bathrooms, mop the floors, vacuum… it requires everyone to participate. Some people enter treated completely unfamiliar with cleaning skills and have to be taught the basics. They have to be taught to load a dishwasher, run the washing machine, or clean a bathroom. This is Jesse's job. He makes sure that the cleaning is thorough and teaches the people who do not already have skills. The logic behind double scrub and chores is to teach people how to be self-sufficient and take care of themselves as they leave treatment and move on to their own homes. It also reflects a bias toward order and away from chaos. A using lifestyle is chaotic and their homes and cars usually reflect this by being unkempt and in disarray. In fact, people who do not believe in a Higher Power in the Twelve Step program are often taught that GOD = Good Orderly Direction.

Predictably, there are clients who are lazy, get other people to do their chores, do their chores badly, or do not do them at all! This is aggravating for the house as a whole because the television is off until double scrub is complete. This motivates clients to cover for the lazy people and do their chores for them so they can move on with the day and watch the movie they have picked out. Ultimately, though, it generates resentment that will show up later in house conflicts over something minor. Jesse's well aware of this, having been though treatment himself, so watches as carefully as he can to try to head off resentment before it can get started even if that means putting the lazy guy/gal on "front street," which is embarrassing.

Clients who have "programmed" before, either in prison or in other treatment settings usually take care of business pretty efficiently. They already know the power of group influence, and that chore completion is inevitable so they might as well just take care of it. However clients like Kevin will struggle with it for various reasons, either perfectionism or anxiety or incompetence, which is Kevin's M.O. He is assigned a bathroom today, and predictably he can't find the cleaning materials he needs, claims there are no sponges left, and complains about the smell so he can't breathe when he has to scrub the bathtub.

Jesse is handing him a roll of paper towels, when he catches Angel giving Kevin a really nasty look. "*Oh, shit,*" Jesse thinks.

"Man, why don't you just shut the f**k up and do what you have to do?" Angel snarls.

Kevin looks at Jesse with a pleading look.

Jesse intervenes, "Angel, dude, I know it's irritating to listen to him complain. But it's temporary."

"Why can't he just handle his business? Why do you have to defend him?" Angel asks.

Jesse thinks a minute, "I'm not defending him. I am admitting he's being irritating. But keep it right-sized man, it's just double scrub. It's not that important. Take a breath."

Angel nods and takes a breath. "Okay, but I gotta work some-where away from him."

"You got it. You can help Paul take out the trash."

Angel nods and leaves the area.

"Do you really think I am irritating?" Kevin wonders to Jesse.

"Well, you have asked for help at least 4 times in 15 minutes, and most of what you wanted, like paper towels, you could have found yourself." Jesse admitted. "Kevin, why do you think you do that… act like you are helpless or not very smart?" Jesse asks.

"I never thought about it," Kevin admits. "It's just the way I am."

"You know, I am not so sure that's true, man. I think you might find it easier to let other people do stuff for you. But, the tradeoff is you never get to feel in control. I'm not so sure that's such a good way to run your life."

Kevin seemed to be thinking about this.

"Are you going home after treatment?" Jesse asks.

"I figured so. I need to get a job."

"Have you thought about an SLE? I am wondering if it might be better for you to get some independence and not live with your parents."

Kevin had never thought about this. "I thought the SLE was for people who didn't have anywhere else to go?"

"No, it's for people to move into a recovery-supportive environment while they go back to school or go to work. It gives them structure while they are getting on their feet. Maybe you can talk about this with Janet in your one-on-one," Jesse suggests.

Jesse hears shouting in the kitchen, so turns and hurries across the house. As he enters the kitchen door he sees Raul squared off with Angel, who's holding a trash bag and is furious."

"Stop it!" Jesse shouts. "Stop it or I roll you both up now."

The men take a step back and look at him.

"That Motherf**ker ate my enchiladas, man! What the f**k!" Angel gestures to his empty Tupperware dish.

"You don't know it was me, homes! How come you're going off on me like that? Do you know who the f**k I am?"

"I don't give a shit who you are in there, ass-wipe! You are the only person in this place with the balls to eat my shit! No one else is that stupid!" Angel glowers.

Jesse moves forward, and tells Raul to step outside. "Take a break — just go have a cigarette. I'll deal with you in a minute." Jesse directs. Raul gives another hater look at Angel and leaves.

Angel looks at Jesse. "My mother and sister brought those for me yesterday! Who the f**k does he thinks he is?"

"Okay, man, that was wrong. I get it, and it would piss me off, too. It's really disrespectful," Jesse agrees. "You're having a tough morning, a lot of aggravation. And so far you haven't put your hands on anyone and you could never have done that if you were loaded."

"Not yet! Why shouldn't I kick his ass?" Angel asks. "Should I just let him punk me like that?"

"Okay, this is a serious deal for you, Angel. You already can't see your son because of a restraining order. You have a decision to make at this point. Do you do what you have always done, and get the same result, or do you do something new?" Jesse challenges him.

Angel looks calmer but not totally convinced. "What's more important to you? Your freedom with the possibility of seeing your son, or the ass-wipe?" Jesse asks.

Angel nods. "Okay, I don't kick his ass. But I feel really stressed out."

"I can see that. You have only been out 6 days. It's a lot to take in, and you have to manage what's coming up for you without being loaded. I really get it. Why don't you give it a rest, and go hang out in your room for a while where it's quiet. Maybe you can write or draw in you journal. I noticed that you like to draw the other day when I saw one of your handouts."

Angel nods and hands Jesse the trash bag, and heads back to his room. This was Jesse's cue to go outside and talk to Raul. But Raul isn't in the smoking area and Jesse can feel his heart start beating faster. He quickly checks the exercise room, the laundry room, and lounge, and then Raul's room. Raul's coat and small bag are gone. Jesse goes to the front door, and looks outside, and there's no sign of him. He had obviously come into the house while Jesse and Angel were talking, grabbed his things, and taken off.

"*Dammit, Raul,*" Jesse thinks, "*You didn't have to run. We would've worked it out.*" However, now that Raul was AWOL there would be a warrant out and eventually parole would catch up with him. Jesse always wondered if that's what people like Raul, who are "important" in prison culture really want to have happen anyway. The truth is, Angel would NOT have faced Raul off like that in prison. He would have had to be somewhat deferential. Raul must have felt really powerless in that moment, and had to run back to a familiar place where he knows the rules and is in charge of enforcing them.

Jesse checks the rest of the house, checks in with Keisha, then goes to fill out an incident report and document Raul's absence. He then leaves a message for the Clinical Director who calls and instructs him to leave a message for Raul's parole agent. Two runners in one week is hard on the clients and the stability of the house. Jesse documents in the log well enough so that Janet will be able to fill out Raul's discharge paperwork in the morning. Its lunch time, so Jesse decides to call everyone into the dining area, and talk to them about what has happened. Once everyone is in, Jesse begins.

"You probably heard some yelling earlier, right?" he asks. Everyone nods.

"Well, Raul ate Angels' enchilada's and Angel had a "feeling" about that," everyone smiles.

"Unfortunately, I think Raul thought I was going to roll him up, which was not my attention, so he took off."

"Raul's gone?" Karen asks.

Jesse nods. "Yeah, that seems to have been his decision. Here's what I want you to hear. We've had two people run this week, Frankie and Raul, and I know that can make the vibe around here a little weird. If you start to feel like your back is against a wall, you have a choice to talk about it rather than act on it. As addicts, myself included, we always run. Recovery gives us a chance to do it differently and find out things really can work out. This is especially true if we ask for help. Got it?"

Everyone nods.

"Okay, get some lunch and if you want to talk about anything this afternoon just let me know. We have our outside meeting at 4:00, so you have lots of time to rest, do your assignments (which makes them roll their eyes) or your laundry. You can also talk to me, okay? Thank guys." Jesse concludes.

The next few hours are uneventful. Jesse plays a few rounds of spades with the clients, watches some TV in the lounge, studies a little in the office. It's time to get the clients ready for their outside meeting, so he heads to the exercise room to round up any stragglers. He immediately spots Marla and Paul in a passionate embrace too preoccupied to hear him. "*Ah shit,*" he thinks. "*These people are getting more than I am and they're locked up!*"

"Excuse me," Jesse coughs. They break apart quickly, glancing at each other trying to figure out a plausible story. Of course, Paul is first to try.

"Oh, Jesse, I'm glad to see you," Paul says. "Marla here was crying and I wasn't sure what to do so I hugged her."

Marla looked far from tearful. In fact she looked pretty flushed and wide awake.

"That so?" Jesse asks her.

"That's right. I came out here to be alone because I was sad, and Paul happened to come in and find me. He was trying to comfort me." Marla offers.

"Well, I can tell you what I saw," Jesse begins. "I saw the two of you going at it for some mutual comforting, and you know that's not cool. I'm not going to go all 'judgy' on you, but I think you both have relationships, right?"

They both look sheepish.

"Okay, it's time for the outside meeting, so you need to get your things. Please sit apart in the van and at the meeting. In fact, I'm going to set a non-com (non-communication) contract on you both until Janet and Ricardo get here and decide what to do. Got it?"

They nod, and go inside.

Jesse goes to the office and calls Janet for some advice. She answers on the second ring.

"What's up, Jesse?" Janet answers.

"I'm sorry to bother you. It's kind of wild this weekend. I just caught Paul and Marla in the clenches and Keisha and I are on duty. I've put them on a non-com until you and Ricardo get in tomorrow. Is there anything else I should do?"

"Sounds to me that you got it handled. I was headed out to a meeting anyway. Where're you going? I could meet you there and help you keep them out of each other's pants," Janet offers.

Jesse sounds relieved. "Are you sure it would be okay with you? It's your day off."

"I live to serve, bubba. Count me in," Janet laughs.

Jesse caught Janet at a good time. She wasn't really going to a meeting, she was crocheting, and wallowing in front of the TV in her PJ's since she was too depressed to go out. This was a Sunday pattern since David left. At first she did this because she was too destroyed to do anything else and for some weird reason Law and Order comforted her. More specifically, Criminal Intent. It was probably the absence of romance that made her so comfortable. Goren was so "Aspergery" that he never even flirts! Unfortunately it has become her fallback plan when she hasn't scheduled anything else and it often leaves her depressed on Monday morning. She NEEDS a meeting, and sees Jesse's call as a nudge from God to get off her ass. "God does for us what we cannot do for ourselves," she giggles as she puts on some clothes.

When she arrives at the church Jesse, Keisha and the clients are already seated. Janet does a quick head count and notices that Raul is missing. She nods to Jesse and settles in the back row near the bathroom to catch them if they try to step out and smoke or hook up. Scary as it is, dealers sometimes target NA and AA meetings knowing that they might be able to take advantage of someone who's struggling.

Sitting in the meeting she notes the worn-looking woman across from her with ill-fitting dentures and the handsome tattooed Mexican guy next to her. Nearby is the sweet old guy with 30 years sober and the computer nerd guy next to him. There's a hard-looking biker chick sitting next to a soccer mom, and the big, red-faced jackass over by the coffee urn. She feels an overwhelming desire to hum, "Which one of these things is not like the other" and finds she is grinning stupidly to herself. This is her tribe, these are her "peeps," and she settles back in the metallic, cold chair feeling warmer than any other place she can sit.

MONDAY

Janet arrives a little early and opens up the log. She notes the incident with Karen's return and pregnancy, Amanda and her boyfriend, Angel and Kevin, Angel and Raul, Raul's absence, and Paul and Marla. She also sees that Kym met with Carolyn and Franks, Marla and Gary, and that Mike's graduation was uneventful. Sarah notes that Marla and Paul were following the non-com and that Marla went to bed early. Probably hiding.

Women's Group

The energy in women's group feels heavy today. This isn't surprising given the weekend Amanda, Marla and Karen had. Janet opens the group with a family day check-in. Carolyn is the first to speak. "My husband didn't serve me papers," Carolyn smiles.

"Did you expect him to?" Janet asks.

"I wasn't sure. He was so angry when he brought me here that he didn't speak to me until Saturday."

"That can feel like a long time," Janet agrees. "What did he say?"

"He seems to understand that I am depressed, though I could tell he wants me to be "fixed" in a hurry."

"I can relate to that," Marla offers. "Gary is already pushing to get me home and this is only my second week!" she says resentfully.

"You sound angry about that," Janet observes.

"Because he wants me home to control me, not because he cares about me."

"Why does he say he wants you home?"

"Something about it feeling more like a home when I am there. Probably because I'm the maid," Marla blurts with disgust. "And you guys are making such a big deal about a hug that I can't even talk to my best friend here."

"You mean Paul?" Janet clarifies.

"Yes, of course Paul. I'm on this stupid non-com thing. You are just as controlling as my husband!" Marla says with indignation.

Janet is taken aback, but like Kym on Saturday thinks, *"Oh THERE you are!"*

"I have to say Marla that this is the most energy I have seen from you the whole time you have been here. Do you always get this riled when you're told 'no'?"

"It's not about that! It's about being wrongly accused and punished for no reason!"

"With your permission, I am going to ask the other women for input in case they are seeing something I'm not seeing about the situation. It's important to me that I not 'jump to conclusions' and treat you fairly, okay?" Janet asks.

Marla nods.

"Ladies, I need your help. When I see Marla and Paul together, I feel a vibe between them that's more than just friendship. I'm not judging it, but I'm trying to fill in the BLIND Square that we learned about last week in Psychoed. You live with them. What do you see?"

Laura is tentative but speaks up. "Honestly, Marla, I notice your eyes light up and you laugh more with Paul than you do the rest of us. I notice that you always sit with him in group."

"I don't blame you at all, Marla. He is a really great guy and makes all of us laugh," Carolyn adds.

Karen notes, "I think Paul likes a lot of attention, especially from women. I feel kind of sorry for his fiancée, because if he's doing this thing with you in rehab, he'll probably do it with other women out there. I know his type, I've dated them."

Laura chimes back in. "When I was miserable with my husband,

I started to notice other men and compared them to my husband. The more I compared them, the worse my husband looked."

"Like building a case to leave him?" Janet asks, "I've done that!"

The women all smile.

"Okay, you guys. I think I hear what you're trying to tell me," Marla says. "You think I am into Paul because he's paying attention to me and my marriage sucks."

The women nod.

Marla looks at Janet, "Okay, I sort of buy that. But what do I do? I still like the guy and my marriage still sucks?" she asks, as everyone laughs.

Amanda raises her hand. "I really messed up this weekend," she says with tears in her eyes.

"You mean with Todd?" Janet asks.

"Yeah. I knew it was wrong, but he really wanted it and I knew it wouldn't take very long and it would make him happy."

"Were you afraid he wouldn't see you anymore if you told him no?" Karen asks. "Because I do that which is why I think I am pregnant. I didn't make Brent use protection because he says he hates the way condoms feel."

Amanda nods. "I really need Todd to help me when I get my baby back. What if I lose him?" she asks.

"What if you don't get your baby back because you're so worried about how Todd feels?" Janet asks, a little too sharply.

Amanda looks hurt.

"I'm sorry about the way that came out, Amanda. It was harsher than I meant it to be. I'm worried that you lose your focus, which you say is being a mother."

"I don't know if I should be a mother at all," Karen says. "It looks really stressful to have everything put into place for support."

"I want to be a mother!" Amanda states. "I want to stay focused. Maybe Todd shouldn't come and visit for a while?"

Janet smiles at her. "That's probably wise. Will that be hard for you?"

"Yes," Amanda admits. "But I am not strong enough to tell him no yet, so it's better not to be in that position, I think."

The women all nod in unison. The group talks about self-care for a few minutes longer and then breaks up so they can get ready for Community group.

Community Group

Ricardo, Janet and Jorge all lead Community group. The mood's a little tense, which would be natural after such a hectic weekend. Everyone does their check-in and the group opens for concerns. "I have a concern," Paul starts. "I feel like Marla and I are getting singled out, when other people 'over-associate' too, by your definition."

"I'm aware that you and Marla feel picked on, like we're over-reacting." Janet says, ignoring his attempt to throw other people under the bus.

"And you are!" Paul says heatedly. "We're not in f**king High School, and you shouldn't be the hall monitor!" It was interesting to see the less-charming side of Paul, and Janet's hoping that Marla is noticing the similarities between Paul's behavior and the behavior her husband demonstrates on a regular basis.

Ricardo looked down unable to meet Janet's eyes. "*I guess I'm on my own,*" she thinks.

"Paul, when you live with people 24 hours a day you can get really close in a really short time. This can be a kind of blind spot – you can get really attached, too attached, before you even know it. It is also normal to try to feel good by starting a new relationship."

"That's bullshit. I already have a relationship – I'm engaged!" Paul states.

"Paul you may not be seeing the situation objectively because you're in it. That happens to everyone which is why counselors don't counsel themselves or family members. We're too close. Is it possible that you are too close to this situation to see it?" Janet questions. She is throwing him a rope – a face-saving way out of the confrontation.

Thankfully, he takes it.

"Okay, maybe. But I think you guys are making more of the situation than it is. I certainly wouldn't break off my engagement because of my friendship with Marla. I'm not trying to break up her marriage either."

Janet could feel the slight intake of breath from Marla who was sitting next to her. Janet's heart went out to her. Despite her denials, Marla really HAD begun to put more into the relationship than she knew. The other women were aware of this after the women's group that morning.

"You are such a douche!" Karen shouts. "Men like you are the reason women become bitter."

Paul curls his lip, "Women like you, maybe?"

Janet interrupts. "Okay, Okay. You know character assassination is not acceptable here. It needs to stop."

Karen and Paul stay quiet.

"Obviously, there's a lot of feeling here, and the hour is about up. I would encourage you all to write in your journals, and we can tackle this again in psychoeducation group. Ricardo and I will find the right topic. Let's take a break and we'll see you back here in a few," Janet says.

Janet and Ricardo walk into the office. "Jesus that was intense!" Ricardo exclaims. "How do you always know what to say when that shit jumps off?" he asks in admiration.

Janet looks at him and says, "Paul and Marla are not our only problem. This was a wild weekend, and we both have some damage control to do. I need your help Ricardo," Janet says.

Ricardo sits down and gives her his full attention.

Janet lists:

- Karen is pregnant and has a decision to make
- Jesse caught Amanda and her boyfriend having a quickie on the side of the house. I need to decide what to do. Do I tell her CPS worker about her rule violation? It's a significant one.
- Raul ate Angels enchiladas, they got into it, and Raul bounced
- Paul and Marla were making out in the exercise room. They are in a non-com right now, but we need to get a strategy.

Ricardo thinks for a moment then answers Janet's concerns. "Well, Karen's on your caseload, so I guess you'll hear more about her thinking now that she's had a couple of days. I don't think we should exit Amanda or call CPS like we're the sex police, but maybe her boyfriend shouldn't come to family group next week. If Raul bounced, I guess we just have to call his parole agent. I'm not sure what to do with Paul and Marla. You saw this coming last week, and you've already talked to Marla once, right?"

Janet has been listening to him. "There's a note here that Sarah processed with Karen on Saturday evening, so I can get more info from her before I meet with Karen. Karen seemed okay in women's group. I don't want to tell CPS about Amanda, but I am struggling with the fact that this is obviously a sign that her impulse control is still not well managed. I'm more worried about what it means than the sex part. Actually, she suggested herself that Todd not come to visit for a while, which is a good sign. It says in the log that Jesse left a message for Raul's P.O. so I think I just need to do his discharge paperwork. You're right, I talked to Marla and she was pretty feisty in group this morning and mad at us for the non-com. The other women gave her some great feedback so I think she is starting to see her part. You can see that Paul's pretty pissed off too. Did you see Marla's face when he said he would never break up his engagement for her? Poor baby," Janet sympathizes. "Boy, Karen sure has Paul's number! I wonder what happened in the couple's session Kym had with Marla and her husband. Maybe something there set her off –"

Ricardo interrupts, "Or maybe she's just lookin' to change the way she feels. It happens all the time. Sex'll do that for a minute. Paul really gets to me. He's mister charm, but no recognition that he hurts people."

"Yes, like Marla, in this case," Janet adds "At least she got to see his nasty side. Don't think I won't help her notice that in our next one-on-one."

"Do you think the guy's a narcissist? He really seems to love himself enough," Ricardo observes.

"What an ironic question," Janet thinks to herself. "That's a great Kym question. We can ask her at Clinical Staffing. The problem is that if they continue down this slippery slope, the whole house is going to be affected."

"Okay, I have to do psychoed in a few minutes. Let's let the non-com stand for now and talk about it with the team. It would be easier if we caught them in bed - we could just discharge them. This feels a little greyer to me," Ricardo suggests.

Janet nods. "It feels grey to me too. I like that suggestion, thanks Ricardo. What are you teaching about today?"

Ricardo is looking at the curriculum and Janet sees a smile spread across his face. "We're taking about Acceptance," Ricardo laughs.

"Perfect," Janet smiles.

Clinical Staffing

The staff starts arriving for Clinical Staffing, the one time a week when everyone is in the same room. The Clinical Director plops down at the head of table and reads the log book to get oriented.

"Has Raul's PO been called?" he asks no one in particular.

"Yes, sir," Janet answers.

Jesse arrives with his usual McDonald's bag and gives Janet a fist bump. Keisha and Sarah trail in, followed by Jorge and Carl.

Kym arrives loaded down with totes. "I decided to donate some of the unused art supplies my son won't touch so the guys can have art stuff even when it is not Art Therapy day."

"What a great idea!" Janet exclaims. Then she remembers her own collage in her desk. *The collapse of civilization* is her pet name for it at this point. Maybe she'll take it to therapy today.

Ricardo sees Carl and can't resist teasing Janet, "Janet, I think there might be something on your chair. I don't want you to get it on you."

"Really, what?" she asks while looking at her seat. Then she spies Carl, who is oblivious, and suppresses a giggle. She makes a face at Ricardo, who grins.

"I have so much to tell you," Kym announces.

"Well, if we do this in order of immediacy, I think we need to deal with the Paul and Marla situation," the Clinical Director suggests. "Kym, what did you notice in your session with Marla and her husband on Saturday?"

"They are really conflictual... distrusting... a lot of damage there. I did bring up the SLE and while he was resistant at first, he started to move in that direction. She seemed relieved it might be an option."

"So the marriage is really in trouble. Do you think she's hoping Paul might be a solution?" he asks.

"Well, the look on her face in Community when he announced he would never leave his fiancée put the kibosh on that fantasy," Janet observes. "She looked wounded, so I think you're right. The women gave her some great feedback in group this morning, so I think she's starting to see it more realistically."

"The guy was a real prick in Community," Ricardo says. "That reminds me, Kym. Do you think Paul might be narcissistic? The guy doesn't seem to notice or care who he hurts."

"That's a great question," Kym thinks aloud. "He certainly does spin things his way, uses charm instead of work to get his way, tends to be entitled, doesn't take negative feedback well or being told no. Was he hostile in community?"

"Yes, he had a nasty tone of voice," Jorge says.

"Hmmm. He could be. Sometimes people are narcissistically defended, but not characterologically narcissistic. This means he might have learned narcissistic defense mechanisms from one of his parents, but has more capacity for empathy than an actual narcissist."

"Unless he was acting, he seemed to get some insight about how his fiancée might be seeing him during assignment group on Friday." Janet offers.

"Why does this matter?" the Clinical Director interrupted irritably. "Does it change what we would do with the two of them?" he challenges.

"Right now they are on the non-com from Sunday," Jesse says. "If he blew her off in Community, it may be that she takes the hint and things may cool down on their own."

"We can't leave it up to them because I don't trust Paul not to charm his way back in, and she's pretty vulnerable. I think it's just entertainment for him, a way to get a rush." Janet says.

"When does Paul graduate anyway? He's been here a while," the Clinical Director asks.

"He is finishing his Relapse Prevention packet now, so he can leave as early as Saturday if we don't extend him," Ricardo says looking at Paul's chart.

"I think that may be best for all concerned. Ricardo, can you have a one-on-one with him today and talk to him about it? I don't want him to feel we're tossing him out, and at the same time we need to head this thing off," the Clinical Director offers.

"Does the non-com stand?" Ricardo asks.

"I think it does," the Clinical Director decides. "However, let's soften it to be no private communication, but they can communicate in group settings so the house doesn't get all funky."

"I think that's a good call, "Janet echoes. "I will also meet with Marla and process Community group with her."

"Okay, that takes care of that! So what do you want to do about Amanda and the CPS, Janet?" the Clinical Director asks.

"You know, the more I think about it the more I think we're on top of the situation and her incident with Todd was just another impulsive behavior she needs to change. She's willing to be in solution, so I think we let it be for now, other than suspend her boyfriend visits."

Kym smiled at her. "I agree. Oh, I had an encounter with Kevin's mom that could shed some insight on the development question you asked me, Janet. She was worried about his sleep and suggested getting some Ambien from HER doctor to help him through."

"Seriously?" Keisha exclaims. "Isn't he here for prescription med abuse?"

Kym laughs. "Indeed he is. Clearly the disease concept I've been teaching about isn't making a dent! I did explain that we were encouraging him to use non-pill solutions. She agreed, but seemed a little doubtful."

"That explains why he came to talk to me later!" Jesse says. "He was worried that he could get sick or psychotic if he wasn't sleeping enough, and wanted to know how he would know if he is psychotic!" Jesse laughs.

"He looks like he's sleeping every time I do rounds," Carl says.

"That's what I told him! He says he only looks like he is sleeping. On the other hand, he was pissing Angel off during double scrub with his whining, and we got to have a real conversation about his "playing dumb" behavior. I suggested that he consider an SLE instead of going home after treatment."

"Was he open to it?" Janet asks curiously.

"He seemed to think about it."

"Well, we would have to get parental buy in," Kym mentions. "I can talk to them next Saturday if you want me to," she offers.

"I think it would be useful to see what they might be thinking," the Clinical Director agrees. "What's going on with Karen and the pregnancy?"

"I was able to spend some time with her on Saturday," Sarah offers. "She's been thinking about county programs for support, but childcare would be a problem if she went to work or school. She's afraid her folks may not help. She has been afraid to ask them, so I suggested that maybe Kym could meet with the family to support her."

"I'd be happy to." Kym says. "What about the father of the child?"

"He's not in the picture," Sarah continues. "She's more worried about the damage she may have done to the fetus when using meth. She didn't know she was pregnant when she was using. I suggested she meet with an OB/GYN and talk about it."

"I let her use the phone to make an appointment this morning," Jorge offers.

"Wow, she's being proactive. That's a good sign," Janet notes. "She seemed to be thinking realistically in women's group this morning. It's a tough decision to make. It sounds you did a great job with her Sarah," Janet adds.

Sarah smiles.

"How are the clients doing with two AWOLs last week?" the Clinical Director asks curiously "Did it come up in Family group?" he asks Kym.

"No, they had other things on their mind. We were normalizing chaos in change, and Mike did a great piece of work with Laura's mother. The clients are so generous with their experience with other people's family members. There's no 'charge' so it can be an open conversation."

"Honestly, I think they are relieved Raul's gone even though no one says so. The house feels lighter somehow." Jesse offers.

"I noticed that when I first walked in this morning," Ricardo says. "Maybe everyone was holding their breath a little, even if we didn't know it."

"I knew it," Janet admits. "I have a hard time with the more institutionalized guys. I get defensive just anticipating the push against my boundaries even if they aren't doing it yet!" she adds.

Ricardo laughed, "You're the one telling me not to personalize Angel's lying!"

Janet smiles. "We teach what we need to learn, right? I read that somewhere," and everyone laughs with her.

Process Group

Janet slips out of the Clinical Staffing to facilitate the Process Group. Community group had ended with strong feelings floating in the air, so it will be important to address unfinished business as quickly as possible. As the clients wandered in, she could feel the unease. In general, addicts and alcoholics have neither skill nor practice with conflict resolution. They're normally protected from their feelings by the effects of the substances, and often their reactivity is a by-product of poor impulse control and the fact that they are controlled by their fight-flight-freeze reactions. In fact, due to early trauma and broken early attachments, some of the clients were emotionally flooded before they ever had language to describe their feelings, consequently they are missing an emotional vocabulary. That's why treatment programs often use "Feeling Faces" handouts to teach clients what to call the physical sensations they are having. Their physical reaction and facial expression indicates a feeling that the Feeling Faces help them to identify and label.

Marla looks as though she has retreated and left her body, which worries Janet.

"Marla? What's going on?" she asks tentatively.

"I'm not sure," Marla answers listlessly. "I don't feel very much at all."

"Well on the outside you appear to be low energy and like you aren't really here."

"My husband said on Saturday that I would look like that at home. I thought it was just the alcohol."

"That probably made it worse, it's true." Janet probes further, "But can you tell me what happened, maybe earlier today that has taken your energy away?"

"I'm not sure. It just feels like all the fight has gone out of me; like it's hard to care about anything."

"Hmmmmm. Like you lost hope?" Janet wonders. She doesn't want to push Marla to talk about her feelings about Paul in a group setting which might be too exposing for her.

"I suppose so," Marla mutters.

Janet addresses the group. "Sometimes when strong feelings jump off, like at Community Group today, it triggers our childhood feelings about anger. Some of us get mad and want to attack what's making us uncomfortable, (Janet gestures with her hands moving forward); some of us want to run away from it (Janet pulls her hands back towards her); Some of us want to check out completely (Janet indicates leaving the top of her head). All three of these are natural responses to strong emotion. Can anyone relate to these?" she asks.

"I can relate to attacking," Karen says. "I went all 'emo' on Paul," she observes.

"I definitely attacked you, Janet," Paul chimes in. "I was out of line, and had no call to be such a dick to you."

"Maybe you aren't a narcissist after all," she thinks to herself.

"Thanks, Paul, for owning it," Janet smiles

"So, I guess what I did was the checking it out thing because when I get scared I get really still. Like sometimes when my husband is yelling at me, it seems far away like I am watching him from somewhere. I never actually get up, even though some part of me knows I should leave," Marla says.

"And I really wanted to get up and leave, but I thought I'd get in trouble," says Amanda.

"Were you feeling overwhelmed?" asks Janet.

"It's like my chest gets hot and all I can think of is, 'I have to get out of here.'"

Janet nods.

"Strong emotion triggers the fight or flight system, technically the sympathetic nervous system, and our heart rate goes up, our breathing is faster and more shallow, our blood floods out to our outer extremities, our blood pressure shoots up… we are READY for something to happen." Janet explains.

"What other physical changes happen when you have strong emotions?" Janet prompts.

"My throat closes up when I feel like I'm going to cry — so I can't talk," says Marla.

"My neck and shoulders get really tight," says Angel.

"When that happens it gets harder for some of us to think, like we are being flooded" Janet adds.

Janet sees nods around the room. "I see that you know what I mean."

"So our best bet is to bring down our emotional temperature to ease the flooded feeling and be able to think again. What kinds of things could you do?" she asks the group.

"I can walk away," suggests Kevin.

"I can count to ten," says Laura.

"I can say I need to take a time out," says Karen.

"Those are all excellent suggestions!" Janet responds.

The group continues in this vein and the tension in the room eases noticeably. It is so important for the clients to learn to use their words to address conflict rather than act out. Janet is proud of them.

After group Janet decides to meet with Marla individually to see where her head is.

Marla

"Marla, you did a great job in group today. I really appreciated your willingness to hang in there and try to figure out what you were feeling. You were struggling in Community this morning"

"It's been a very long day. This Paul thing has really taken a lot of my energy."

"I saw your face when he pointed out that he would never leave his fiancée for you. You looked pretty hurt, though you hid it quickly."

"I guess. I guess I was making more of it than it really is."

"Do you think you may have wanted him to rescue you from your husband, Gary?"

"That would be pretty juvenile, huh?"

"It's more like you don't think you can rescue you by yourself. It makes me think you might not be feeling very strong right now," Janet offers.

"No, I feel pretty broken, actually. I get overwhelmed when I think about leaving and going back to my old life. Kym mentioned the SLE, maybe buy me more time."

"What do you think about that suggestion?"

"Gary didn't seem happy about it."

"I am asking you about YOUR thoughts, Marla. What do you think is best for you?"

"I think I need more time."

"I think you're right," Janet smiled. "See, you do know what's best for you. I talked to the team, and we've decided to lift the non-com with Paul for all group situations, but we ask you to honor it by not being alone with him."

"Oh, that's fine," Marla agrees. "That wasn't a good idea anyway. Now if I avoid him I can blame it on you!" she smiled.

Janet wraps up with Marla and stops by her desk to grab her purse on the way to her own therapy. Ricardo is charting, and looks up at her."

"How did it go? Did you meet with Marla?" he asks.

"It went really well. I think she's relieved she can avoid being alone with Paul and blame it on us," she smiled. "What did Paul say?"

"He thinks we are over-reacting, but agreed to non-com alone with her. He is fine with finishing on Saturday, and suggested that Kym meet with him and his fiancée so they can be on the same page for his discharge plan. He wants her to have realistic expectations."

"Hmmmm," Janet pondered, "do you think he's laying ground-work for forgiveness if he uses again?"

"That's a great point! It wouldn't surprise me. How do you think of that shit?" Ricardo asks.

"I am very long in the tooth, and grey with time, grasshopper!" she laughs. "I'll see you in the morning."

Janet

Janet arrives at her therapist's office about 5 minutes late, with her collage folded in her purse. She unfolds it, revealing it's starkness to her therapist.

"This was my collage in art group last week, and needless to say I didn't stay in the group and 'share'."

"Well, it's pretty grey, almost skeletal," her therapist observes.

"Hmmm. Skeletal. Just the bones. Honestly, that's how it feels sometimes. Like all the fluid has been drained out of me and I feel desiccated, like those cow heads in the desert."

"Are there exceptions to that feeling? Times when you almost feel alive?"

Janet thinks. "Yes, when I'm running a really good group or being silly with Ricardo," she smiles.

"What is it about those times?"

"I feel useful, I am part of something bigger than myself. I step out of me and I am in service or have perspective. I'm not stuck in the hamster wheel in my head."

"So you feel like you matter, instead of disposable like you felt with David?"

"Exactly. I know I'm 'supposed' to feel like I matter just because I love myself enough, but right now I don't. I feel like I matter when I have something to offer that matters. It sounds so codependent when I say it like that!"

Her therapist shrugs. "Existentially, we have to find our purpose here and then participate in it. You found a purpose in your sobriety when you almost died. There's nothing codependent about that. The part that worries me is that you don't feel alive when you are alone. It speaks to your need for self-care and nurturing. Act as if you are lovable, treat yourself like you matter, and eventually you might feel it."

"You sound like my sponsor – 'act as if'," Janet laughs.

"You're sponsor sounds very wise," her therapist laughs with her.

Glossary

Some of my readers may not be familiar with Treatment Center staffing patterns and treatment abbreviations, so I have included a glossary.

CD Tech: The Chemical Dependency Technician is an entry level position, usually someone in recovery. They assist with program structure, client transportation to appointments, and oversight of the community as a whole.

Lead Counselor: This is usually a senior counselor with the most education and experience, and often serves to support the clinical decision-making and case management of the other counselors while carrying his/her own caseload.

Clinical Director: This is usually someone who started in the counseling role, and has advanced in his/her education and experience to take clinical responsibility for the structure, program development, and clinical quality of the program. They do chart review, teach in-services, and provide clinical guidance to the staff.

Counselor: They are usually certified counselors, and are able to perform the 12 Core Functions: Screening, Intake, Orientation, Assessment, Treatment Planning, Counseling, Education, Case Management, Report and Record Keeping, Consultation, Crisis Intervention, and Referral.

CD Intern: They are usually in a supervised practicum at a local alcohol and drug counseling training site, and have to complete 255 hours of on-site experience for their certification.

Hospitals and Institutions: H&I is a service program of Alcoholics and Narcotics Anonymous where member's volunteer to conduct meetings in places where addicts and alcoholics are confined. They "bring the meeting."